"In this outstanding book, Dr. Jim teaches us that God offers marketplace Christians more than a rule book of timeless business principles. More than rules and principles, God has invited us into a personal friendship and partnership with Him through His Holy Spirit, Who will empower and lead us into all truth concerning our personal and professional lives. Through this highly practical guidebook, Dr. Jim already has helped me to yield more control of my business over to the Holy Spirit, 'Our Unfair Advantage' in the marketplace."

Darren Shearer
Host, Theology of Business Podcast
Author, *Marketing Like Jesus*

"*Our Unfair Advantage* caused me to assess the heart and health of my leadership motivation, methods, and practice to reveal where I was missing the mark or conflicted with Scripture. More importantly, it graciously, yet compellingly charts a clear path for me to be even more on-purpose."

Kevin W. McCarthy
Author, *The On-Purpose Person* and
The On-Purpose Business Person

"The question, 'What is leading you' — or, who is leading your business decisions and life — is a critical question to ask. At FCCI, Fellowship of Companies for Christ International, we encourage people to seek a greater purpose for their life and business. Jim has nailed that approach to business by helping us to focus on an audience of one."

Terence Chatmon, President & CEO,
Fellowship of Companies for Christ International (FCCI)

"In *Our Unfair Advantage,* Dr. Jim describes in detail how we can utilize the gift of the Holy Spirit in the very intimate details of our businesses each and every day. Filled with a step-by-step introduction to utilizing the power of the Holy Spirit, this book will move your spiritual life and your business life to a higher level."

Jim Brangenberg
Founder & Host, iWork4Him Business Radio

"You can expect your work-life to experience a transformational shift as you apply Dr. Jim's teaching on how to participate with the Holy Spirit as an Unfair Advantage."

Leray Heyne, President & CEO,
Windows of Heaven (Jesus' Storehouse)

"For too long, we've locked God's Holy Spirit in a Sunday-morning box with no concept of the tremendous advantage He could offer in the marketplace. But that changes now. In *Our Unfair Advantage,* Dr. Jim demystifies the role of the Holy Spirit in your professional life and gives practical principles to unleash His power to transform your business. Prepare to move from being swayed by what everyone else is doing, to being intimately led by the One who will set you leaps and bounds above the rest."

Kyle Winkler
Author, *Silence Satan*
Creator, the *Shut Up, Devil!* App

OUR

UNFAIR
ADVANTAGE

**UNLEASH THE POWER
OF THE HOLY SPIRIT IN YOUR BUSINESS**

DR. JIM HARRIS

HIGH BRIDGE BOOKS
HOUSTON

Our Unfair Advantage:
Unleash the Power of the Holy Spirit in Your Business
by Dr. Jim Harris

© 2015 by Dr. Jim Harris

High Bridge Books' titles may be purchased in bulk for educational, business, fund-raising, or sales promotional use. For information please contact High Bridge Books via www.HighBridgeBooks.com/contact.

Published in Houston, Texas by High Bridge Books

Cover design by Matt Arnold

All definitions are taken from Merriam-Webster, Incorporated Copyright © 2015 digital app.

Bible quotations are taken from *The New King James Bible* via The Bible Study App for Mac Version 5.4.3 (5.4.3.1) Copyright © 1998-2013 Olive Tree Bible Software.

Printed in the United States of America

ISBN (Paperback): 978-1-940024-47-9
ISBN (eBook): 978-1-940024-48-6

CONTENTS

ACKNOWLEDGMENTS

First and foremost, I thank God, my Savior Jesus, and the Holy Spirit for guiding me in the writing of this book. My only desire is to record faithfully Your words and be Your pen. May this book be pleasing unto You.

To my wife and eternal partner, Brenda, who has matured into an unstoppable spiritual warrior. Without you and your endless support, I could not fulfill my calling from the Lord. I'll proudly hold your hand all the way to heaven!

A special thanks to my good friend and spiritual brother, Kyle Winkler, whose calm spirit, deep knowledge, and consistent witness has guided, taught, and encouraged me for many years.

A huge shout out to Pastors Arnie McCall, Buford Lipscomb, and Rick & Jennifer Curry for their spiritual mentoring and guidance through severe trials, accelerated spiritual growth, and glorious encounters with the Holy Spirit.

Thanks also to my spiritual mentors and close brothers in Christ—Ben Watts, Tony Chavez, and Steve Jones.

Thank you Darren Shearer of High Bridge Books for your phenomenal editing, book publishing, and marketing efforts. You are indeed the best!

Finally, a very special thank you to Pastor Keith Moore of Faith Life Church located in Branson, MO and Sarasota, FL. In just two years, your sermon series and Word Life Supply ministry has grown my faith exponentially beyond anything I learned in my previous 60 years of church. Much of this book was revealed to me through applying your teachings. I am eternally grateful to you and for your ministry.

*To those who deeply desire to
glorify God in their businesses.*

INTRODUCTION

If you work in a for-profit firm whose leadership desires to glorify God in their business, this book is for you!

The target audience for this book is what I call 2%ers. A 2%er is any man or woman who works in a for-profit, privately-held, Biblically-based company.

As a 2%er, you have available to you an unlimited, amazing, and exciting unfair competitive advantage in your market that, until now, you likely have been underutilizing.

The purpose of this book is to help you unwrap and unleash your unfair competitive advantage in business for the glory of God!

Musician Keith Green once said,

> "If anyone writes a great story, people praise the author, not the pen. People don't say, 'Oh what an incredible pen… where can I get a pen like this so I can write great stories?' Well. I am just a pen in the hands of the Lord. He is the author. All praise should go to him."

Just like Keith, I am just a pen.

Whatever impact this book has on your life, give the Lord all the glory!

~Dr. Jim

CHAPTER 1

WHAT LEADS YOU?

"And if it seems evil to you to serve the Lord, choose for yourselves this day whom you will serve, whether the gods which your fathers served that were on the other side of the River, or the gods of the Amorites, in whose land you dwell. But as for me and my house, we will serve the Lord."

~Joshua 24:15

Everybody is led by something. Whether it is obvious to you or not, you are currently—right now—being led by something.

Something is at the helm of your ship, guiding your direction, setting your course, and ultimately impacting your life.

As a child, parents or guardians likely are the ones who fed you, gave you shelter and clothes, and taught you what was acceptable and expected. They protected you, nurtured you, and sometimes even spoiled you. They were the ones who primarily led you in your early, formative years.

As you began attending school, you quickly learned that more people were now involved in leading you. You were forced to learn new and sometimes uncomfortable truths about how to live with others outside your immediate family and neighborhood.

This outside influence continued to grow as you entered high school and, perhaps, college. You were being led by many voices that were sending mixed signals to you and applying various levels of pressure to influence your behavior.

Before you knew it, you were thrown into the "real world" where dozens of voices desired to lead you... from bosses, fiancés, spouses, customers, marketers, and so many more.

The point: you and I are led by something. And whatever you decide to be led by has a profound—if not permanent—impact on your life... including your business life.

As the owner of this book, you are likely a leader in your business. Whether you are at the top, in the middle, or even in the trenches, you influence others. Therefore, you indeed have leadership impact and potential.

WHAT A LEADER DOES

As of this writing (6/17/15), Amazon.com lists...

- 4,303,934 results for "business books"
- 178,180 results for "leadership books"
- 25,511 results for "business leadership"
- 744 new releases in "Last 90 days" and 180 "Coming Soon"

I guarantee the vast majority of these books—98% or more—share someone's five, seven, ten, or even 21 critical qualities, skills, or competencies for how a leader should lead others. They share their secrets of best practices that you can use to become a leader just like them.

Over the last 30 years, I've read thousands of books and articles on leadership. As I scan my library of the best of the best, reflecting on their content and key points, so many sound and look exactly the same. Most of them are filled with exactly the same ideas and concepts, just stated in slightly different ways.

Should I even mention the number of daily blogs, tweets, and posts that tell us what a great leader does? Guess I just did.

We simply are overwhelmed with what others say, think, or proclaim to be *the* way to be the leader everyone needs today.

These often interesting and occasionally profound works focus on one critical question: What does a leader do?

That is exactly the wrong question. What a leader does (his behavior, communication style, decision-making ability, etc.) is not the most critical element you need to know. There is a far more profound and necessary question that no one is asking.

THE RIGHT QUESTION

As I scan all the available leadership writings and teachings, I cannot find any that directly address the right question.

The answer to the right question inevitably determines the destiny of not only the leader but also the destinies of everyone they lead.

> The right question: What leads the leader?

The right question: What leads the leader?

Let's get personal. Have you ever...

- Thought about what makes you the leader you are?
- Stepped back to assess what you rely upon in your leadership?
- Stopped long enough to reflect on what really leads you?

That which leads you, in the end, is released in your leadership and in your role in your business.

What leads you is at the fundamental core of your ability to work, succeed, and leave a legacy.

At the risk of sensationalism or ringing an unnecessary alarm, you must ask and decide: In the end, what leads you? Then and only then can you make the right determination to continue on that road or on a potentially more exciting and profound basis for your leadership.

Before I ask you to make a potentially radical and life-changing leadership move, let's look at some of the most common ways leaders are led.

DR. JIM HARRIS

1.1. Nine Common Ways Business Leaders Are Led

It would be easy to list 100 or more ways business leaders are led, but they typically fall under one of the following categories.

Here is what I call the "What Leads You" list. It is comprised of the most prominent leader-led types I've seen over my more than 30 years in business.

Note: During the writing of this book, I asked my blog readers to comment on expressions they've heard leaders say that reflect each category. I've included just a few of the comments. Each commenter will receive a free copy of the book. See… it pays to sign up for my blog and contribute at www.DrJimHarris.com.

1: Head-led

Head-led leaders analyze everything. They seek more knowledge, information, reports, and analysis. They rely on logic and spreadsheets to make their final decisions. Head-led leaders often find themselves over-relying on their ability to analyze and think critically as their primary go-to style.

Head-led business leaders say things like…

- "That's a great idea. Let's do it."
- "Let's run one more report."
- "Numbers don't lie. What do the numbers say?"
- "Why hadn't I thought of that?"
- "I like the way you think."
- "Show me the numbers. We make decisions by knowing, not guessing." ~Curt Fowler, blog commentator

– 5 –

2: Money-led

Money-led leaders focus on the amount of money to be made or lost. Wall Street is rabidly money-led. Making money is an absolute necessity in a for-profit business. However, money-led leaders allow cash flow, profit, and margins to be *the* overriding factors in almost every business decision.

Money-led business leaders say things like...

- "We'll make a ton of money on this."
- "I love these margins."
- "How can we cut more costs?"
- "How can we squeeze another 1%-2% margin into this contract?"
- "I don't care about earnings quality. Numbers are numbers, and I want to make mine."
  ~Sidney Bostian, blog commentator

3: Innovation-led

Innovation-led leaders constantly seek the latest technological, digital, or creative platform to grow the business. They are enamored, even giddy, over the latest upgrade, app, software, website, marketing technique, or unique concept. Although improvements are obviously necessary to any sustainable business, innovation-led leaders often push for anything that is the "new thing."

Innovation-led business leaders say things like...

- "What would Steve Jobs or Apple do?"
- "We gotta upgrade now, or we can lose market share, customer loyalty, and...!"
- "Innovate or die!"

- "Sometimes we have to lead our customers where they need to go... even when they don't want to go."
- "This will be so cool!"
- "What about this is new and exciting?"
  ~Jason Pyne, blog commentator

4: Opportunity-led

Opportunity-led leaders enthusiastically jump into any reasonable open door in front of them. They fix their sights on the next big break, strategic alliance, or unexpected offering that could take their business to a higher level.

Opportunity-led business leaders say things like...

- "We better jump on this while we can."
- "No way we can let this opportunity slide by."
- "Wow! What an open door! Let's go!"
- "Sure, this opportunity is a little outside of the vision of our company, but I think it will be worth the effort." ~Curt Fowler, blog commentator
- "The more we throw against the wall, the more will stick." ~Sharon Kendrew, blog commentator
- "I know that if I just go for it... it will happen!" ~Jesus Estrada, blog commentator

5: Price-led

Price-led leaders are a close cousin to money-led leaders—with this one caveat: Rather than focusing primarily on how much money they can make, price-led leaders look for the cheapest price, squeezing every cent they can out of the other guy's hands.

Price-led leaders say things like...

- "You need to really sharpen your pencil on this."
- "This is the best option because they're the cheapest." ~Darren Shearer, blog commentator
- "Hey, any sale is a good sale." ~Aric Johnson, blog commentator
- "Everything is negotiable." ~Howard Drake, blog commentator
- "We want it cheap and good!" ~Angeline Teoh, blog commentator

6: Expert-led

An expert-led leader is enamored quickly by the latest management or leadership fad, always looking for the new, great concept from a speaker, author, or advisor. Expert-led leaders often implement the "new" business concept quickly without taking the time to assess how—or even if—it should be adopted and integrated into their operations.

Yes, including this one stings a little because I speak, write, and coach professionals for a living, but it is still true.

Expert-led leaders say things like...

- "So & So Magazine had a featured article that says..."
- "Here's a great idea from the conference... Let's do it!"
- "Our competitor is reading this guy's book... Here's your copy."
- "The entire industry is doing this."
- "Let's find the best expert in the field and get him or her in here."

- "According to [insert trendy management fad writer], shouldn't we do it this way instead?" ~Jason Pyne, blog commentator

7: Pressure-led

Pressure-led leaders claim to work better in emergency, urgency, or crisis situations. They often succumb to both inside pressures (i.e. emergencies, deadlines, etc.) as well as outside pressures (i.e. community, political, supply chain, etc.). When not putting themselves under pressure, pressure-led leaders sometimes unintentionally place unnecessary and irrelevant pressures on others.

Pressure-led business leaders say things like...

- "Gotta hit the deadline."
- "Get it done now... or else."
- "No excuses."
- "Time is money."
- "Failure is not an option."
- "I don't care how we do it, but we've got to get it done now!" ~Jason Pyne, blog commentator
- "Put the pedal to the metal!" ~Robins Duncan, blog commentator
- "We're just gonna put our heads down and grind this baby out! We can sleep when we make it." ~Aric Johnson, blog commentator

8: Feelings-led

Feelings-led leaders constantly assess their feelings and emotions before they make a move. By no means wimps, pressure-led leaders are deeply moved and overwhelmed by feelings of fear, anxiety, excitement, comfort, or safety. They constantly assess how they "feel" about something.

Feelings-led leaders often say things like...

- "This just doesn't feel right to me."
- "My heart is not in this."
- "This is going to hurt."
- "Man, I've never been more excited about something."
- "This really makes me happy!"
- "Don't rock the boat." ~Darren Shearer, blog commentator
- "It's better to be safe than sorry!" ~Robins Duncan, blog commentator
- "This could really be our big break." ~Chris Bier, blog commentator

9: Pride-led

Pride-led leaders see themselves and their companies as special, different, and unique. They take themselves and everything they do quite seriously. Pride-led leaders often refuse to back down to anyone or any group—even when they are wrong.

Pride-led business leaders say things like...

- "We're different."
- "They can try that. We don't need to."
- "We know what is happening in the field. You stay here in the office and keep working."
- "I don't want to hear it!"
- "It is my way or the highway." ~Howard Drake, blog commentator

Honesty Check

As you read these, I am sure you quickly saw others who fit one or more of these types. The more important question is, "Where do you see yourself?"

Here is your first book assignment. Place a check in the boxes that most accurately describe what leads you.

- ☐ Head-led
- ☐ Money-led
- ☐ Innovation-led
- ☑ Opportunity-led
- ☐ Price-led
- ☑ Expert-led
- ☐ Pressure-led
- ☐ Feelings-led
- ☐ Pride-led

1.2. THE FRIGHTENING REALITY

At one time or another, one or more of the things on the "What Leads You" list has led us. Frankly, most of us are a combination of several of these things most of the time.

But now, you need to consider this. Every one of the nine categories is exactly how 95% or more of every secular, for-profit company is led!

Don't move past this too fast. Just take another moment to let this sink in.

These nine categories are simple examples of how the traditional business world around the globe leads.

In one word, the world is led by the "What." For them, it is all about the idea, money, opportunity, innovation, price, experts, etc. These categories are the ones upon which many secular businessmen and businesswomen lean to make their decisions, to drive their businesses, and ultimately to reach their goals.

Unfortunately, the vast majority of us—2%ers (men and women leading for-profit, privately-held, Biblically-based firms)—are no different!

We are very likely led by the exact same things as our secular counterparts. Why?

We have equal access to all the same business magazines, gurus, books, analysis, and market information controlled by the world's system as do our competitors. Therefore, we are just as vulnerable as they are to succumbing to the overwhelming temptations to lead our companies in the exact same way.

The world's business ways are so prevalent, pervasive, and substantial that they make it nearly impossible not to be led by them.

Now, here is the frightening reality.

If you are led by the ways of the business world, you have absolutely zero competitive advantage over your competitors!

Zero advantage. None. Does not exist.

If you only rely on your head, opportunities the world puts in front of you, or any combination of the rest of the list and more, you are on the same battlefield, fighting with the same tools and resources. No distinct competitive advantage!

I can hear you asking, "So, Dr. Jim... are you telling me I'm not supposed to use my head or look at opportunities or think about the financial aspects of my work? Is that what you are saying?"

No, no, no, no! Again... no!

God gave you a brain and a sound mind. He gave it to you so you can reason and think and plan and grow. He gave you feelings to build your sensitivity to others. He expects you to use them.

> *If you are led by the ways of the business world, you have absolutely zero competitive advantage over your competitors!*

What I am boldly challenging you to do is make a big shift, a shift toward unleashing your unfair competitive advantage in your market.

Why is this shift unfair? Why is it a distinct competitive advantage?

Because it is based upon one and only one thing: from you being led by the What...

> *"Do not love the world or the things in the world. If anyone loves the world, the love of the Father is not in him. For all that is in the world—the lust of the flesh, the lust of the eyes, and the pride of life—is not of the Father but is of the world." (1 John 2:15-16)*

...to being led by the Who!

> *"For as many as are led by the Spirit of God, these are sons of God." (Romans 8:14)*

CHAPTER 2

THE BIG SHIFT

"And I will pray the Father, and He will give you another Helper, that He may abide with you forever—the Spirit of truth, whom the world cannot receive, because it neither sees Him nor knows Him; but you know Him, for He dwells with you and will be in you."

~John 14:16-17

As a 2%er, you need to be led by the Holy Spirit. Period.

Nothing else.

It's a big shift—a HUGE shift—from being led by what the world expects to what the Spirit offers.

It's a monumental leadership transformation to go from being Head-led, Money-led, Innovation-led, Opportunity-led, Price-led, Pressure-led, Feelings-led, and Pride-led to being fully and only Spirit-led.

It's a shift the world (non-believing business leaders) do not understand, not because they are incapable of it, but simply because they are not believers. They cannot receive the potential unfair competitive advantage because the Spirit of God is not living in them.

Just think about a few of the shifts you may need to make.

From	To
Externally-led	Spirit-led
Follow society & current trends	Follow the Word & eternal truths
Be politically correct	Be Biblically aligned
Driven by success	Called by God
Submitting to the spirit of this world	Unleashing the Spirit of God

And these are only the beginning.

As you begin the big shift, it's important to review the two most fundamental ways God leads you.

> *"For it is written, 'Man shall not live by bread alone, but by every word that proceeds from the mouth of God.'" (Matthew 4:4)*

> *"He who heeds the word wisely will find good."*
> *(Proverbs 16:20)*

The first way God leads you is through His Word. His perfect, infallible Word teaches, inspires, convicts, encourages, corrects, and so much more.

I sense no reason to belabor this truth because, by reading this book, you likely believe the power of the Word.

It all begins with the Word of God.

> *"For as many as are led by the Spirit of God, these are sons of God... The Spirit Himself **bears witness with** our spirit that we are children of God." (Romans 8:14, 16)*

The second fundamental way God leads you is through His Holy Spirit. This passage is worth your considerable, in-depth study far beyond the duration and intent of this book.

Yet it is important to take a quick dive into a key phrase inside Romans 8:16: "The Spirit himself *bears witness with* our spirit..." We'll come back to this phrase often in the rest of the book. Here is why it is so critical to *the big shift*.

When you were born again, your dead spirit from birth was reborn. Now, you have both your reborn spirit and the Holy Spirit of God living inside you. Your spirit, therefore, bears witness with the Holy Spirit inside you.

"Bears witness with" literally means we have a co-witness living inside us, the presence of God upon whom we can call upon, seek out, ask, inquire of, and be led by anytime... anywhere.

May we agree on one critically important fact? That is... when you receive the Holy Spirit, He is far more than just a "Get-Out-of-Hell-Free" card. Sadly, millions of believers—many of whom are in business today—think all God wants for us is just to save us from hell.

Even with the hundreds of wonderful lists, articles, and Bible studies available in churches, bookstores, and on the internet that explore the many ways the Holy Spirit teaches, guides, speaks, protects, and is working through us, very few believers are taught much beyond the Holy Spirit being their one-way ticket into heaven.

Even fewer of us have been taught, trained, or encouraged on how to be more Spirit-led in our businesses and professional lives.

Yet the Spirit is ready, willing, and able to be your co-witness in all facets of your professional life.

2.1. IS IT POSSIBLE?

"To him the doorkeeper opens, and the sheep hear his voice; and he calls his own sheep by name and leads them out. And when he brings out his own sheep, he goes before them; and the sheep follow him, for they know his voice." (John 10:3-4)

Global economy. Demanding customers. Unrelenting pressure to do more, make more, and cut costs. Dog-eat-dog market mentality.

Is it really possible for you to be led by the Holy Spirit in today's global business world?

The answer is a resounding YES!

It is more than possible; it is well within your reach.

The Spirit of God filled the entire Bible to overflowing with accounts of men and women who were led. The Spirit spoke to and led...

- Abraham to get ready to move,
- Moses from a bush to get ready to lead the people out of Egypt,
- Joshua to conquer the Promised Land,
- Nehemiah to rebuild the walls of Jerusalem in record time,
- Esther to boldly approach the King, risking her life in the process,
- Ruth to cling to the God of Naomi and forsake her family,
- David to defeat Goliath and become a great King of Israel,
- Solomon to lead the Israelites with wisdom,
- Elijah to defeat the false prophets of Baal,

- Elisha to boldly request a double-portion of Elijah's spirit,
- Jonah to preach the word and redeem a hostile land,
- Joseph and Mary to get married and birth the Son of God conceived out of wedlock,
- Simeon and Anna to be in the temple at exactly the time when Joseph presented Jesus,
- Luke to write the Gospel that bears his name,
- Peter to preach the first recorded sermon in the New Testament, saving over 3,000 souls,
- Ananias to go to Saul, the enemy of the saints in Jerusalem,
- Paul… in virtually everything he did,
- John to write Revelation,
- …and so many more!

These are just a few of the hundreds of the Biblical examples of men and women led by the Spirit of God.

Even the Son of God said,

"'Most assuredly, I say to you, the Son can do nothing of Himself, but what He sees the Father do; for whatever He does, the Son also does in like manner.'" (John 5:19)

Frankly, as a 2%er, you are no different. You have the exact same Spirit living inside you.

Is it possible to be led by the Spirit in business today?

Oh, yes. It only takes a mustard seed of faith (Matthew 17:20) to make the big shift!

2.2. WHY SHIFT TO *THE WHO*?

Here are six powerful reasons to go ahead and make the big shift.

1: The Spirit knows the mind of God.

"But as it is written: 'Eye has not seen, nor ear heard, Nor have entered into the heart of man, The things which God has prepared for those who love Him.' But God has revealed them to us through His Spirit. For the Spirit searches all things, yes, the deep things of God. For what man knows the things of a man except the spirit of the man which is in him? Even so no one knows the things of God except the Spirit of God."
(1 Corinthians 2:9-11)

Many of us think it's cool to attend a conference with a world-famous CEO or leadership guru speaking. It can be a great experience to sit under the instruction of a great person as we tap into their wisdom and experience. There is nothing inherently wrong about listening to any noteworthy expert in business. My precaution to you is to filter always everything they say or write through the Word and the Witness.

Imagine, however, for every situation, challenge, obstacle, opportunity, or decision you face… rather than seeking the human guru in front of you, you seek the mind of God inside you!

Whew! There is no comparison between these two options.

Give me the deep things of God for how He desires me to run my business over anyone else's insights… every time!

2: The Spirit freely gives to us God's wisdom for our businesses.

"Now we have received, not the spirit of the world, but the Spirit who is from God, that we might know the things that have been freely given to us by God." (1 Corinthians 2:12)

God already has revealed to the Spirit all His wisdom and plans for you and your business, even the things you have no way of understanding in your head. The Spirit can reveal them to you as He wills and if you ask.

Even more, this advice is totally free! The advice already lives inside the Spirit who bears witness with your Spirit. All you need to do is ask. (Much more on how to do that later. I am not going to leave you hanging.)

3: The Spirit knows all truth.

"However, when He, the Spirit of truth, has come, He will guide you into all truth; for He will not speak on His own authority, but whatever He hears He will speak." (John 16:13a)

As a 2%er, you already have living inside you the most powerful consultancy this universe will ever know. You can be guided in all truth for your business, your employees and colleagues, your vendors and suppliers, your customers and community members... anyone your business touches.

The Spirit never lies, never fudges the truth, never misleads, never understates, and never misses anything you need to know. More so, leveraging the Spirit for the truth will set you free (John 8:32) to become everything God wills for your business.

4: The Spirit knows the future of your business.

"...and He will tell you things to come." (John 16:13b)

Did you catch that?

Did you *really* catch that?

Imagine having a consultant available to you 24/7/365 that already knows everything that is ahead of you in your business for tomorrow and into forever.

Oh, my!

This is not to say the Spirit will text or email you the Top 10 news or financial insights every morning. He will, however, in His perfect timing, guide and lead you one step at a time in the path you need to take in order to fulfill your calling through your business.

Sometimes, God's instructions through the Spirit make no logical sense:

- Sacrifice your son on the mountain. (Genesis 22:9)
- Walk around the city for seven days, blowing your trumpets. (Joshua 6:3-4)
- Dip yourself in the river seven times to get clean. (2 Kings 5:10)
- Rub spit and mud in your eyes to see again. (Mark 8:23)

In these cases and in so many more, what the Spirit said to do made no sense, yet those willing to follow the Spirit always triumphed, always won, and always were blessed.

5: The Spirit leads you to abundance.

"Blessed shall be the fruit of your body, the produce of your ground and the increase of your herds, the increase of your cattle and the offspring of your flocks. Blessed shall be your basket and your kneading bowl. Blessed shall you be when you come in, and blessed shall you be when you go out. And the Lord will grant you plenty of goods, in the fruit of your body, in the increase of your livestock, and in the produce of your ground, in the land of which the Lord swore to your fathers to give you. The Lord will open to you His good treasure, the heavens, to give the rain to your land in its season, and to bless all the work of your hand. You shall lend to many nations, but you shall not borrow."
(Deuteronomy 28:4-6, 11-12)

God is a God of plenty, of increase… not of scarcity or of decrease. His desire is to bless His children.

The Spirit will only guide you in the best path, to the best employees, to the best customers, and to the best opportunities. He will steer you away from loss, bad deals, and wrong partnerships or alliances.

The Spirit will never take you down the wrong road where you or your company could get ruined.

Never.

Only by following the lead of enemy will you open yourself up to decay and ruin.

6: The Spirit is your #1 Advisor, Consultant, and Coach.

"Trust in the Lord with all your heart, and lean not on your own understanding. In all your ways acknowledge Him, and He shall direct your paths." (Proverbs 3: 5-6)

When you decide to make the shift (and I sense you are already), the Spirit will tell you when you should…

- Go
- Stay
- Stop
- Build
- Invest
- Align
- Avoid
- Defer
- Wait
- Expand
- Move
- Prepare
- Hire
- Fire
- Buy
- Sell
- Run!

The Spirit is and should always be your #1 Business Advisor, Consultant, and Coach.

(I pray I might make your list one day at #5 or #6 or #7!)

2.3. Your Real Enemy

"The thief does not come except to steal, and to kill, and to destroy."
~John 10:10a

Your real enemy at work is not your competitors, suppliers, banks, or your employees.

Your real enemy is not the market conditions, global competition, or lack of cash flow.

Your real enemy is Satan!

He is the one who will do everything he can to defeat, distract, and derail you from being led by the voice of God through His direct connection to you, the Holy Spirit.

Satan desperately wants you to be led by the world, by what he controls (Ephesians 2:2).

God desperately wants you to be led by his Spirit, what He controls (Romans 8:14-16).

> *"For we do not wrestle against flesh and blood, but against principalities, against powers, against the rulers of the darkness of this age, against spiritual hosts of wickedness in the heavenly places." (Ephesians 6:12)*

It's time to turn your attention to the real battle you face at work.

It's the same battle you face at home: the battle of right versus wrong, of good versus evil.

It's time to remind the enemy he already has lost, that he was defeated 2,000 years ago at the cross.

It's time to tell him he does not control or influence you in your business, for you are now being led by the Spirit.

It's time to tell him that, at the name of Jesus, he must flee! (James 4:7)

2.4. YOUR GREATEST BUSINESS DECISION EVER

"And do not be conformed to this world, but be transformed by the renewing of your mind, that you may prove what is that good and acceptable and perfect will of God."

~Romans 12:2

The greatest business decision you will ever make is to be a Spirit-led leader.

No other business decision you will ever make will...

- Excite and enliven your spirit to a higher level
- Be more challenging to implement and integrate into your daily life
- Unleash greater spiritual power throughout your organization
- Be more misunderstood, even mocked, by family, friends, employees, and customers
- Pack greater earthly and eternal rewards
- Be fought harder by the enemy and his army

Will you be a Spirit-led leader or continue to be a world-led leader?

When compared to any other decision you will make, this one stands above and beyond all others.

It even bears consequence on what Jesus will testify in your defense to the Father on your day of judgment.

The question is, "Will you be a Spirit-led leader or continue to be a world-led leader?"

I know you have already decided. My Spirit senses you are ready to make *the big shift.*

But before you do, you must prepare yourself for the inevitable roadblocks just ahead.

CHAPTER 3

ROADBLOCKS

"We are hard-pressed on every side, yet not crushed; we are perplexed, but not in despair; persecuted, but not forsaken; struck down, but not destroyed."

~2 Corinthians 4:8-9

Paul knew the trials he would face for preaching the gospel. Yet they did not deter him from fulfill his calling from the Lord.

Am I suggesting you are to face beatings, imprisonment, shipwrecks, and more by making this *big shift*? No, of course not. Yet it would be dishonest if not outright misleading to suggest there are no roadblocks to make the shift toward becoming Spirit-led in business.

When the Lord called me to leave secular speaking and consulting five years ago to rebrand and refocus my business toward glorifying Him in business, trust me... there were challenges.

Many speakers' bureaus with whom I'd been one of their most popular and sought after speakers suddenly dropped me like a hot potato.

Potential clients ran because of fear that I might come in and try to "gospelize" their company.

My new market, 2%ers, for the most part did not know me as a believer in business with a new, fresh message.

Up to that point, all my keynotes, books, training materials, blogs, and everything else I had created over the previous 20 years was secular-based even though I occasionally injected a hint of the Word whenever appropriate.

I basically had to start from scratch as a 57-year old with a start-up, home-based advising firm.

Part of my testimony is that, even though I had to scratch out an existence for the next few years, God provided everything we needed. We never missed a mortgage payment, a meal, our son's school tuition, or anything else we needed (Philippians 4:19).

Will your testimony be as dramatic? I pray not.

Yet the decision to move fully into a Spirit-led business life does have its roadblocks.

I am therefore compelled to share the major roadblocks I faced and ones you likely are to face as you make the big shift. I am likewise compelled to share the one key I have learned that helps to overcome every roadblock to becoming a Spirit-led leader in business.

3.1. IT'S NOT NATURAL

"But the natural man does not receive the things of the Spirit of God, for they are foolishness to him; nor can he know them, because they are spiritually discerned. But he who is spiritual judges all things, yet he himself is rightly judged by no one. For 'who has known the mind of the Lord that he may instruct Him?' But we have the mind of Christ."

~1 Corinthians 2:14

You and I most likely have been programmed to do business a certain way: the way of the world.

We've attended endless seminars and training sessions, read books and articles, listened to speakers and bosses who rambled on and on about on how to...

- Make decisions (head-led)
- Assess upside and downside risk (opportunity-led)
- Increase profit and decrease costs (money-led)
- Push the latest productivity-increasing systems and software (innovation-led)
- Integrate the latest business fad (expert-led)
- Make the fast, shoot-from-the-hip decisions leaders are expected to make (pressure-led)

With years, even decades of world-based, business brainwashing, it is not natural in our flesh to step back and call upon the Holy Spirit to show us the best way to go.

At first, embracing our unfair advantage will feel unnatural. That's okay. All positive change, at first, feels unnatural (i.e. starting an exercise routine, dieting, time-blocking your schedule, moving from Windows-based computers to Mac, and even upgrading to a new software).

That's okay. Once you get started and see success, it will become second nature.

Are you ready to move beyond the natural into the supernatural?

3.2. IT'S NOT OBVIOUS

*"But Martha was distracted with much serving, and she approached
Him and said, 'Lord, do You not care that my sister has left me to serve
alone? Therefore tell her to help me.'"*

~Luke 10:38

Let's step inside Martha's head for minute.

It was obvious to Martha that a sense of urgency was needed
to get the meal ready for all the guests. Big crowd. Jesus teaching.
People getting hungry.

*There must be a big meal ready for everyone when he finished
teaching... Right? Why couldn't anyone else see the obvious? Especially
my lazy, no-good sister, Mary, who should have been helping from
the start but is out there sitting around and wasting her time listening
to Jesus when there is work to be done! She should know better!*

Martha even went so far as to interrupt Jesus' teaching and
basically told Jesus to tell Mary to get in the kitchen and help.

Imagine having the audacity to interrupt the teaching of Jesus, calling out Mary in front of a big crowd, and then
commanding Jesus (because He obviously would agree with me)
to tell Mary what to do... to get up and help with the meal!

It's so obvious... Right?

It is easy to be led by what appears to be obvious rather than
allowing yourself to be led by the Spirit.

It might seem obvious to...

- Extend paying a vendor a few days to help
  your cash flow crunch
- Fire that employee who is perpetually late to
  work
- Expand into that city with so many people and
  so much potential

- Break the contract of a long-term vendor for a new vendor with a lower price
- Promote the long-term, loyal employee over the high-potential, younger one
- Drop or eliminate the training budget during budget cuts

Being led by the Spirit in business is not always the most obvious thing to do. You must learn how to discern through the Spirit the not-so-obvious and transform it into the obvious.

More on this later.

3.3. IT'S NOT POPULAR

"Then His disciples came and said to Him, 'Do You know that the Pharisees were offended when they heard this saying.'"

~Mathew 15:11

"Then they cried out with a loud voice, stopped their ears, and ran at him with one accord; and they cast him out of the city and stoned him. And the witnesses laid down their clothes at the feet of a young man named Saul."

~Acts 7:57

"But when the Jews from Thessalonica learned that the word of God was preached by Paul at Berea, they came there also and stirred up the crowds."

~Acts 17:13

These rather dramatic verses powerfully point out a raw truth: Not everyone will accept your revelation with open arms and shouts of "Hallelujah!"

Others will have a hard time understanding your revelation about the unfair advantage, even some 2%ers. It goes against the grain of everything they also have been taught.

Some may even scoff. Scoff? Yes, the shift is so potentially unpopular it is common to hear the prototypical put down, "He thinks he hears from God!"

But isn't that exactly the point?

The Bible is one long and powerful story of people who heard from God: Adam, Abraham, Moses, Joseph, Samuel, David, Solomon, Jeremiah, Isaiah, Elisha, all the apostles, and, especially, Jesus himself.

Embracing our unfair advantage may not be popular, but consider yourself in fantastic company even when some doubters or scoffers come your way.

3.4. NOT SURE YOUR FAITH IS STRONG ENOUGH

"Jesus said to him, 'If you can believe, all things are possible to him who believes.' Immediately the father of the child cried out and said with tears, 'Lord, I believe; help my unbelief.'"

~*Matthew 9:23-24*

"Watch and pray, lest you enter into temptation. The spirit indeed is willing, but the flesh is weak."

~*Matthew 26:41*

"But I have prayed for you, that your faith should not fail; and when you have returned to Me, strengthen your brethren."

~*Luke 22:32*

This roadblock is typically one of the most profound and challenging.

Even as an on-fire 2%er, you sometimes doubt yourself and the depth of your faith. You may start comparing yourself to the spiritual giants of the Bible—from Caleb to Paul—and immediately think you fall short… that your faith is not strong enough to succeed.

This is also one of the primary roadblocks the enemy loves to throw at you. He even had the audacity to throw this accusation at Jesus (see Matthew 4:3, 5, 8).

Yet be assured that, if you have even a tiny amount of faith, your faith is strong enough.

> *"So the Lord said, 'If you have faith as a mustard seed, you can say to this mulberry tree, 'Be pulled up by the roots and be planted in the sea,' and it would obey you.'"*
> (Luke 17:4)

Your faith brought you into an eternal relationship with Jesus, a promised eternity alongside Him in heaven.

Your faith is certainly strong enough to become a Spirit-led business leader.

3.5. AFRAID YOU MIGHT GET IT WRONG

"And Peter remembered the word of Jesus who had said to him, 'Before the rooster crows, you will deny Me three times.' So he went out and wept bitterly."

~*Matthew 25:75*

Are you human? Me, too. That means you and I have, at times, fallen short of the glory of God (Romans 3:23).

You've made leadership mistakes in the past. As you begin this new journey, you are likely to make more but not as many, not as frequently, and not as severe.

Even when you do, you are forgiven.

> *"If we confess our sins, He is faithful and just to forgive us our sins and to cleanse us from all unrighteousness."*
> (1 John 1:9)

As you move toward being led by the Spirit of God, sometimes you might miss it, but keep going.

The reason we continue to get it wrong is that we are listening to the wrong spiritual channel!

Pastor Keith Moore loves to teach how God is always talking to us on His channel, so we need to learn to get onto His channel. As Pastor Keith says, "God may be speaking to us on FM, but we are trying to listen on AM." Our job is to learn to tune into His channel, to fine tune our station to His, and stay there!

As we learn to tune into His channel more precisely, we will start getting it right more and more often. In time, we seldom will miss what the Spirit is telling us.

When you learned to ride a bike, you may have scraped your knees a few times in the beginning. But over time, you were cruising down the road with no hands and loving every minute of the ride!

3.6. YOU START STRONG BUT FADE

"So He said, 'Come.' And when Peter had come down out of the boat, he walked on the water to go to Jesus. But when he saw that the wind was boisterous, he was afraid; and beginning to sink he cried out, saying, 'Lord, save me!' And immediately Jesus stretched out His hand and caught him, and said to him, 'O you of little faith, why did you doubt?' And when they got into the boat, the wind ceased."

~Matthew 14:29

Two people walked on the water in the Bible: Jesus and Peter.

Peter started strong. He stepped out of the boat in faith, looked at Jesus, and listened to Jesus. He paid no attention to his surroundings: the raging water, the wind, and the waves.

He started strong and then quickly faded as he took his eyes off Jesus and called out to be saved.

Ever return from a great business conference loaded with great new ideas to implement? Worse yet, have you ever had your boss return from a conference or a vacation loaded down with a big list of new stuff to implement?

In either case, you may start strong in implementing those wonder thoughts, yet more often than not, they quickly fade into the way it's always been done.

It's easy to start strong on a new, exciting adventure. It's especially exciting as a 2%er to begin a new, exciting adventure for the Lord.

This course, however, is different. Once committed, there is no turning back. It is an all-in race to the finish. Just like Paul said,

> *"...so that **I may finish my race** with joy, and the ministry which I received from the Lord Jesus, to testify to the gospel of the grace of God." (Acts 20:24b)*

One of my heroes of the faith is Caleb. His story gets me so pumped up every time I read it, think about it, and study it.

He was 40 years old when he and Joshua tried to convince the Israelites to enter and take the Promised Land (Numbers 14:7). Only he and Joshua survived the 40 years in the desert because Caleb had a different spirit (Numbers 14:24).

At 80 years old, he helped Joshua lead the armies of the Israelites into the Promise Land and conquer kingdom after kingdom. Then, after waiting 45 years, when God instructed Joshua to divide the lands, he offered Caleb any land he wanted.

Caleb's response is a shining example of starting strong and not fading:

> *"And now, behold, the Lord has kept me alive, as He said, these forty-five years, ever since the Lord spoke this word to Moses while Israel wandered in the wilderness; and now, here I am this day, eighty-five years old. As yet* **I am as strong this day as on the day that Moses sent me***; just as my strength was then, so now is my strength for war, both for going out and for coming in. Now therefore,* **give me this mountain** *of which the Lord spoke in that day; for you heard in that day how the Anakim were there, and that the cities were great and fortified. It may be that the Lord will be with me, and I shall be able to drive them out as the Lord said."*
> *(Joshua 14:10-12)*

At 85-years young, Caleb wanted the same country filled with the giants the other 10 spies feared, cowered under, and turned the hearts of Israel into disobedience because of, ultimately causing them to wander in the desert until their deaths.

That's the man I desire to be!

That's the model I desire to emulate!

Caleb is a phenomenal example of how to start strong, stay strong, and not fade.

My business race is far from over. Like you, when I first made the decision to be Spirit-led, I started strong. The pressures, uncertainties, lost business opportunities, and even my flesh tried to creep into and consume my mind with doubts, uncertainty, and discouragement.

But I chose not to be like Peter and look away. I chose to keep my eyes on Jesus and listen to His Spirit.

I chose to finish my race like Paul.

I decided to start strong, stay strong, and not fade… just like Caleb!

My prayer is that you only will get stronger in your Spirit-led business race.

3.7. YOU DON'T KNOW HOW TO DO IT.

"So he, trembling and astonished, said, 'Lord, what do You want me to do?' Then the Lord said to him, 'Arise and go into the city, and you will be told what you must do.'"

~Acts 9:5

Paul did not know how to leverage his newly-found, unfair advantage in his ministry. He had to learn how to use it.

Neither did I when I began to be led by the Spirit in my business. Yet this is the time when you and I can be totally humble toward and most intimately led by the Spirit.

The unleashing of our unfair advantage is a walk of faith over flesh. It is about being led in our businesses by the Spirit of God rather than the spirit of the world. I certainly would never claim to have all the answers on how to do it or even know all the right questions to ask.

But I can show you through my experience what I have learned so far, which is more than enough to jumpstart your journey.

3.8. A KEY TO OVERCOMING YOUR ROADBLOCKS

Roadblock (n): something that stops progress or prevents accomplishment of an objective

Although it's important to recognize the potential roadblocks you may face as you make the switch from world-led to Spirit-led business leader, it is more important to know how to overcome them.

The enemy most often plants roadblocks to unleashing the Holy Spirit in your business. He will use everything in his arsenal to plant little, big, and even overwhelming bumps in the road. He will continue to remind you of the seven roadblocks we've discussed and perhaps a few more for his devious pleasure.

Expect it.

Remember, his roadblocks are most often temporary (unless you allow them to become permanent) and unnecessary distractions (your road is still very drivable).

He will do everything he can to force you back into his game, doing business under his rules.

A key I have learned to overcome these roadblocks is to, first, memorize this powerful verse:

> *"And do not be conformed to this world, but be transformed by the renewing of your mind, that you may prove what is that good and acceptable and perfect will of God." (Romans 12:2)*

Then, I restate it in my own words... something like this:

> *"I am not conformed to the business ways of this world but am transformed by the renewing my mind through*

the Holy Spirit, to lead and live what is that good and acceptable and perfect will of God in my business."

The battle begins in your mind. It begins with whether you are willing to be transformed by the renewing of your mind.

The battle ends when you powerfully unleash the Holy Spirit throughout your business.

Now, let's get you prepared to unleash the Holy Spirit in your business!

CHAPTER 4

HOW TO PREPARE

*"Prepare your outside work, Make it fit for yourself in the field;
And afterward build your house."*

~Proverbs 24:27

To prepare means to…

- Make yourself ready for something that you will be doing, something that you expect to happen
- Make ready beforehand for some purpose, use, or activity
- Put in a proper state of mind
- Plan in advance
- Get ready

I began playing sports at the age of six. From baseball to basketball to golf, I quickly realized that there was much more to being a good player than just showing up for the games. I had to invest the time, energy, and effort to prepare properly if I had any hope of making the team or playing in the game.

When I began playing golf, I fondly remember the initial excitement when my dad bought my first set of clubs: a driver, five iron, nine iron, and a putter. I thought I was now just like my first sports hero, Sam Snead! But I had no clue how to prepare to play my first round.

My dad gently and specifically taught me how to hold the club, the proper swing path, how to aim and focus, and how to follow through. As a former semi-pro baseball player, he knew how critical it was to properly prepare and did a masterful job of launching my love of the game. (Today, I play to an 11 handicap, so I am open to your invitation anytime!)

As I matured, I came to realize even more deeply the absolute necessity of focused, intense preparation to excel in sports and in life.

It is no different for you as you move toward unleashing the power of the Holy Spirit in your business.

You must prepare yourself.

You must invest the time and energy necessary to get your mind and spirit ready for your next step in the journey.

Here are five areas in which you need to prepare to unleash the power of the Holy Spirit in your business.

4.1. IT'S MORE THAN PRAYER

"After they had come to Mysia, they tried to go into Bithynia, but the Spirit did not permit them."

~Acts 16:7

Are you a little shocked at the title of this section? How could anything be more than prayer? Isn't prayer *the* most important thing we do as believers?

Please understand I am NOT discounting the power of prayer in any way! Everything to do with being led by the Spirit in business begins with prayer. Prayer is not and must never be considered some second-tier spiritual business strategy.

Also, understand that, to be fully led by the Spirit of God in business is about more than prayer. Why?

In far too many cases, even with fully-committed 2%ers, prayer is a pre-timed, calendar activity… simply another *to do* on the daily list of activities. Prayer for your business becomes, "Okay, it's 6:45am… time to pray for a few minutes." Check box.

Similarly, prayer for your business often becomes, "Oh no, I forgot… I need to throw up some prayers before I get to work."

At its worst, prayer becomes a desperate, last-minute, "God-please-save-our-ship" business strategy.

Yes, I raise my hand in confession to all three. How about you?

Even if you and your team invest significant time, energy, and faith into a focused prayer time (and you should), prayer alone is not enough to unleash the complete power of our unfair competitive advantage at work.

Here is an analogy that might help.

God is the engine, the origination of all the power.

Jesus is the ignition, your direct channel of access to the power.

The Holy Spirit is the fuel tank, your personal reservoir of the power.

Prayer is the filling station where you grab the pump and pour into your fuel tank.

Without the fuel, you have no power. Without a full tank of fuel, you only can go so far. Without a properly-connected ignition, you cannot reach the power source.

Even with all these pieces, you still can miss it.

With a filled-up, tuned-up, power-rich vehicle—unless you carefully focus on what is around you and where you are going, watching for the signs and warnings and road hazards around and ahead... unless you are totally aware of your surroundings—your prayer Porsche is bound to stall, get lost, and even wreck.

To prepare to unleash your unfair competitive advantage, it's more than prayer... it's total spiritual awareness!

Be Spiritually Aware

The Holy Spirit is always at work in and around you, in both subtle and blatant ways. Always.

As I stated earlier, it is critical that you fine-tune your spiritual receiver to pick up God's revelations to you through the Holy Spirit channel!

There are two primary levels of spiritual awareness as you prepare to unleash your unfair competitive advantage.

Level 1: Personal Spiritual Awareness

It begins with an intentional examination of how the Spirit is moving within you. You can begin your personal awareness by answering questions like...

- What is the Spirit saying to me today?

- Who is the Spirit telling me to reach out to to-day?
- What do I sense the Spirit is moving me to do in the future?

Take 15 minutes RIGHT NOW to sketch out your responses to these questions. Meditate on them in a quiet place. Why now? This is the first major step in your preparation... to fine tune your receiver to what the Holy Spirit is saying to you. Right now.
Here is some space to jot down your insights.

What is the Spirit saying to me today?

Who is the Spirit telling me to reach out to today?

What do I sense the Spirit is moving me to do in the future?

To become more intentional in your personal spiritual awareness, ask these questions of yourself everyday… more than once.

Level 2: Business Spiritual Awareness

As you develop and refine your personal spiritual awareness, you can then step into intentional focus on your business awareness.

Again, here are a few questions that have helped me become more aware of how the Spirit is moving within and through my business. I ask you to take 15 minutes RIGHT NOW to record your insights about these intentional business spiritual questions.

Where do I sense the Spirit moving in my business?

How is the Spirit moving in this current situation?

Who in and around my business is the Spirit leading?

Colleagues – managers, supervisors, front-line staff, and temporary staff

Customers – local, national, global

Constituents – vendors, suppliers, board of directors, non-customer fans

Community – geographic regions we serve

In what upcoming activities, projects, communications, or business dealings do I need to be more Spirit-led?

The Payoff

In time, as you become more intentional in seeking greater personal and business spiritual awareness, you are taking a huge step forward in being prepared to unleash His power. For now, you know where He is already at work. Ask Him to move as you prepare yourself to move in the direction He has ordained for you and your business.

Often after my intentional prayer times, I literally cry with joy because of how He is impacting those around me for His glory and for allowing me to be a part of His plan!

Candidly, my personal and business spiritual meditations revitalized my commitment to Kingdom impact more than anything else I do.

Through it, I know that I know that I know nothing can stop me!

You see, it is more than prayer. Much more!

When you combine prayer with intentional personal and business spiritual awareness, you have taken the first step toward preparing yourself to unleash your unfair competitive advantage!

4.2. IT'S MORE THAN A VOICE

"So he (Simeon) came by the Spirit into the temple. And when the parents brought in the Child Jesus, to do for Him according to the custom of the law."

~Luke 2:27

"And see now, I [Paul] go bound in the spirit to Jerusalem, not knowing the things that will happen to me there."

~Acts 20:22

Most of us would LOVE for the voice of God to speak audibly to us through a burning bush (Exodus 3:1), a monstrous cloud (Matthew 17:5), or even through a donkey (Numbers 22:28).

There are a few instances in the Bible where people heard the audible voice of God with their physical ears. But these were the exceptions more than the rule. And that is still true today.

Can the Holy Spirit speak to you with an audible voice? Absolutely. Does he do it often? Not in my case, for sure. Why not?

Because He lives inside me! Why then should he have to resort to physically manipulating my eardrums with sounds when He is already inside me, willing and ready to direct me?

Comedienne Lily Tomlin said, "When people talk to God, they call it prayer. When God talks to people, they call it schizophrenia."

That's hilarious... and so true! Makes me want to pen all my prayers with, "Lord, let me be seen as the most schizophrenic business professional in the world!"

God Is Talking to You

Although you very likely believe God is very capable of talking to you, you may catch yourself saying, "I just don't *hear* him. I don't think he's *talking* to me."

Now, some free coaching advice: NEVER SAY THAT AGAIN! NEVER!

Without diving into a deep theological explanation, please trust me when I declare the Lord indeed talks to you. He speaks to you through the Holy Spirit living inside you.

If God is omnipresent, that means He is everywhere, all the time.

If God is omniscient, He knows everything that has happened, is happening, and will ever happen.

If His Spirit is living in you, and He is always around you, then you are surrounded totally by His presence.

Suppose your spouse was always around you, standing beside you everywhere you went, in every meeting you attended, and on every trip you took. Think you'd know it?

Just by her being there, over time, you could sense what she was saying to you… even when she did not speak! (Guys, we've *all* gotten *that* look before. You know what I mean!)

She does not have to speak for her to clearly, distinctly, and powerfully communicate to us.

So how do we know what she is saying even when she does not use words?

In the same way, we hear God speaking to us through an inner knowing.

Inner Knowing

An inner knowing is an internal intuition that goes beyond mental, emotional, or physical senses. It's a spiritual prompting or urge.

You just know. Without hearing an audible voice.

You just know.

Have you ever said to yourself or to someone else, "I *knew* I should not have done that," or "I *knew* I should have done that." Or perhaps, "I *knew* that was a bad decision, but I did it anyway."

How did you know? Who was it that was telling you to do or not to do it?

As a 2%er, it is very likely that your inner knowing came from the Holy Spirit living inside you. It's the same still, small, inaudible voice we seek (1 Kings 19:12).

I urge you not to seek audible voices or burning bushes to hear the Spirit. It's about intentional focus on recognizing your spiritual ear, the one inside your soul.

Later, I'll teach you how to embrace your inner knowing. For now, realize you must seek to connect better with your spiritual ear.

Unleashing your unfair competitive advantage is about far more than hearing a voice.

4.3: BE WHOLEHEARTED

"But My servant Caleb, because he has a different spirit in him and has followed Me fully, I will bring into the land where he went, and his descendants shall inherit it."

~Numbers 14:24

The word, *wholehearted*, means,

- Having or showing no doubt or uncertainty about doing something, supporting someone, etc.
- Completely and sincerely devoted, determined, or enthusiastic
- Marked by complete, earnest commitment
- Free from reserve or hesitation

Caleb is one of my favorite heroes in the Bible. He and Joshua were assigned as two of the 12 spies to search out the Promised Land and bring a report back to Moses. The 10 others were overcome with fear to the point of wanting to kill Joshua and Caleb for exhorting Moses to cross the Jordan and take the land.

Joshua and Caleb, however, believed the Lord's promises and served him with all their hearts, ready to go on the offensive at the Lord's command.

Your journey to unleash the power of the Holy Spirit through you in your business is not for wimps! Once you embrace it, you must proceed with your whole heart, holding nothing back and moving forward as the Spirit leads you.

No Fence-Straddling

"See, I have set before you today life and good, death and evil, in that I command you today to love the Lord your God, to walk in His ways, and

*to keep His commandments, His statutes, and His judgments, that you
may live and multiply; and the Lord your God will bless you in the land
which you go to possess. I call heaven and earth as witnesses today
against you, that I have set before you life and death, blessing and cursing; therefore choose life."*

~Deuteronomy 30:15-16,19

God has given to us a clear choice: His way or the world's way.
He even gave the answer to us.

But it is our choice, not His.

Here is a confession from my professional journey that I pray
helps you.

After being saved as a young teenager, I slowly drifted from
the Lord and the body of Christ. Playing baseball on Sundays rather than attending church started my slow fade at the age of 16.
I was almost 40 years old before I fully came back into the body,
right at the time when I launched my current business.

For the first decade of my new business, I wrote several business books, including some highly-acclaimed works (e.g. Fortune
Magazine Best Business Book, American Management Associa-
tion Spring Selection, etc.).

Then, the Lord began His work on me. Walking purely on
the secular side of business was not where I sensed He wanted
me. So I made the decision to… walk the fence.

For several years, I attempted to keep one foot in the secular
world as I gently reached over the fence and began to place my
other foot in the sacred world of business. I began to speak at pastors' conferences and coach pastoral staffs in solid, biblically-
based management practices. I even preached services when invited.

Although it seemed good enough at the time to be a fence-
straddler, in 2009, the Lord ever-so-clearly said to me (not in an
audible voice but through a powerful inner knowing), "Come
fully over to my side."

It was clear to me that I had to make a choice: either stay in the secular world of professional speaking or jump into the sacred world of business for His glory.

Suffice it to say, even though I took a while (thank God He is indeed long-suffering), I finally did submit and cry out, "Lord... whatever, wherever!"

This was my personal tipping point of complete submission to His will.

This was also my professional tipping point of living whole-heartedly for the Lord though my business.

Your professional journey may be far less dramatic. But the result must be the same... that you joyfully embrace being whole-hearted for the Lord in your business.

Either you are willing to swim in the deep end of the spiritual pool, or you will wade around in the toddlers' pool.

It's your choice. Half-heartedness will be your disaster and downfall.

You know which choice I exhort you to make.

> *"I know your works, that you are neither cold nor hot. I could wish you were cold or hot. So then, because you are lukewarm, and neither cold nor hot, I will vomit you out of My mouth." (Revelation 3:15-16)*

What might fence-straddling in your business look like? It could include...

- Printing a verse on your business card with hopes people will think you are a real Christian
- Cursing one moment then praising God the next
- Trusting the latest industry best-practice rather than God's timeless truths

- Being afraid to pray during the day because someone might see you
- Paying vendors late so you can get your check first
- Treating others in a way you would disdain or be insulted if you were treated likewise

If one of these gives you a gut check, good. They are not intended to insult but to exhort you to seek His will clearly in these and other areas so that you will live wholeheartedly for the Lord in your business.

A Challenge

Now would be a great time to set aside this book—for a day, a week, or more—and invest intentional "rug time" to ask the Lord to prepare your heart to become a wholehearted Caleb in your marketplace!

Go ahead. Close this book. I'll still be here after you determine you are no longer a fence-straddler!

Give It Your All

"And whatever you do, do it heartily, as to the Lord and not to men, knowing that from the Lord you will receive the reward of the inheritance; for you serve the Lord Christ."

~Colossians 3:23

Welcome back! I pray your rug time was a powerful encounter that brought you clarity, peace, and exhilaration.

Now, let's dig into the second piece of how to be wholehearted.

It's simple yet extremely hard. You must now be willing to give it your *all*. I am led to share another personal story to help demonstrate this truth.

I began playing organized baseball at five years old and immediately was enamored with being a pitcher. You are in control. You get to throw the ball hard. Your teammates depend on you. You get more recognition for a win and more blame for a loss than you deserve. I continued pitching in organized leagues well into my twenties. It was more than just a passion.

Growing up in North-Central Kentucky in the late 1960s where basketball reigns supreme, I played basketball primarily to get in shape for baseball season. Although I was a member of a state tournament "Sweet 16" team in high school—a REALLY big deal for Kentucky—baseball was my first love.

I lettered in varsity baseball all four years, ending my career with 23-7 won-loss record. Not bad at all.

During the summer of 1971, the year I graduated, I played in a very competitive summer league along with other top players from around the state. The year-ending tournament was a single-elimination, winner-takes-all event in which we needed to win two games to move on to the regional tournament.

The coach chose me to pitch the first game and for a high school classmate of mine—we'll call him "Steve" although that was not his real name—to pitch the second game. I pitched during the entire game the first night—a long, intense game—and we won. So we drove 40 miles home and returned the next night to play the toughest team in Central Kentucky.

When we arrived at the stadium, Steve was not there. An hour before the game, we learned he decided not to show up to pitch. We never learned why. It really does not matter. I was the best and only remaining starting pitcher on the team. Typically, a starting pitcher gets 3-4 days of rest before starting another game. A pitcher's arm is tired and needs to rejuvenate.

My arm and my body still were tired from the night before.

The coach had no choice but to ask, "Jim, can you go to-night?"

You need to know a little background here. Steve and I played against and with each other for years. We were very friendly competitors, teammates determined to prove to each other and the rest of the community who the better pitcher was. Steve was part of the in-crowd, the cool guy, and I certainly was not. He was a top left-hander with a wicked fastball. I was a right-hander with a wicked curve ball (and a mediocre fastball). As athletes, we had a cool personal relationship but were both totally dedicated to our team winning.

I had never won against the team we were playing that night. Previously, I had lost five games to them over the course of my career in high school and summer leagues. They did not fear me, but I did not fear them either.

So I had plenty of motivation that night! I wanted to beat them, to win two games back-to-back, and to demonstrate who the best teammate was. (Yeah, forgive me for the pride that was showing.)

I started the game, and the entire team was totally pumped to win!

After five innings, we were ahead 4–2. As I stepped out of the dugout toward the mound to start the top of the sixth inning (we only played seven-inning games in this league), the coach asked, "How you doing, Jim?" He could tell I was exhausted, my mediocre fastball was a little weaker, and my curveball was hanging a little higher.

"Of course," I said. "Hey, Coach… I'm fine" and then sprinted to mound as I always did.

He knew what was about to happen and what he would soon need to do. So did I, but I had to give it one last shot.

Well, you can guess what happened. The other team starting pounding me, hitting hard shots all over the park.

In most games like this one, although I was out of energy, I usually was able to get the batter to pop-up, ground-out, or fly-out. Not this time. I was spent.

Pitching 12.5 innings in the last 24 hours in 90-degree weather had taken its toll.

For the first time in the tournament, the other team was now ahead. The coach had no choice but to take me out of the game.

As he walked to the mound, I did something I had never done in my entire sports life.

I started to cry.

Imagine… a just-graduated, 18-year-old high school baseball team MVP with a 23-7 career record, standing on the mound and crying!

Yet I was not ashamed. My tears were from knowing deep inside my soul I had given it my all. I left nothing on the field. I poured out my heart and soul, giving everything I had to my teammates and giving everything I had to win.

But everything I had was not enough… not this time.

The coach took the ball from me and sent me to left field as I always played in the outfield on the days I was not pitching. As I began to step off the mound, instead of my usual trot to my out-field position, I hung my head… and cried.

My shortstop hugged me. My third baseman gave a huge shout of encouragement. The fans applauded me, knowing what had occurred last night and tonight.

I cried all the way to left field and could not stop. Praise God not one ball was hit to me the rest of that inning, for I would not have seen it through the tears.

After the third out, I trotted back into the dugout, still crying though not as dramatically as before. Through deep sniffles and tears, I sat on the bench but was not ashamed. Every teammate came over and thanked me for giving it my all. No condemnation. Only thanks for giving them everything I had.

I thank God again I did not bat that inning; I would not have seen the ball.

Although the final scorecard indicated I was the losing pitcher of record, in a much bigger sense, I was the winner.

As was his custom, the father of my second baseman sat in the stands alongside my dad, who himself was a former semi-pro player. The next day, my dad told me that the second baseman's father, Mr. Jury, who had watched me play alongside with his sons for over a decade, turned to my father and said, "I've never been more proud of Jimmy." (Yeah, my hometown still calls me "Jimmy.")

My dad replied, "Neither have I, Ed. Neither have I."

I tell this story NOT to pump me up in your eyes. Rather, I shared this with you to point out that our Lord will be most proud of you when you serve him wholeheartedly, leaving nothing in your dugout but everything on your business field.

In the end, regardless of what the scoreboard (balance sheet) says, when you serve Him wholeheartedly, you will win, and you will receive the reward of your inheritance (Colossians 3:23).

In your journey to unleash the power of the Holy Spirit though your business, you must purpose in your heart to serve him wholeheartedly!

Therefore, when the Holy Spirit tells you to go or not to go, to buy or not to buy, to sell or not to sell, to sign that contract or not to sign that contract, to hire that person or not to hire that person… whatever He says, do.

Wholeheartedly.

4.4. TRUST IN THE LORD

"Trust in the Lord with all your heart, and lean not on your own under-standing; In all your ways acknowledge Him, And He shall direct your paths."

~Proverbs 3:4-5

WARNING: DO NOT DISMISS THIS TIMELESS TRUTH!

As a 2%er, you've heard this verse hundreds of times. You've probably heard it so often that it would be very easy to just repeat it from rote and not reflect on its deep truths.

We need to camp on this verse for a while, for it's at the heart of unleashing the power of the Holy Spirit in your business.

Let's begin by carefully breaking down this verse's five core components.

Trust in the Lord

Trust is defined as "an assured reliance on the character, ability, strength, or truth of someone or something."

I love the phrase, "assured reliance."

If you are saved, you already trust the Lord for your salvation. You possess the assured reliance that the Lord is true to his promise. You confidently place your trust in Him.

Our trust in the Lord is also an assured reliance that He will indeed be faithful to complete the good work he started in us through our businesses.

With All Your Heart

Here is where so many of us get stuck or hesitate. You'll notice Solomon, writing under the divine anointing of the Holy Spirit, did not say God wants us to...

- "Trust me with all your spreadsheets!"
- "Trust me with all your board of directors!"
- "Trust me with all your market research!"
- "Trust me with all your head!"
- "Trust me with all your feelings!"

The list could go on forever, but you get the point.

It is critical to remind yourself that everything you do in business is all about your heart. It's all about how you allow God to influence, impact, and mold your heart for His glory. Yet, often, the pressures of the business world surround you, your competitors attack you, the marketplace is hostile toward you, your supply chain challenges you, and even your employees may reject you.

It is easy to lose control of our heart and return to our flesh as business leaders. This is exactly why this verse and this practice step is so critical to your success and ultimate significance. Everything comes back to your heart and trusting the Lord with all of it... not just a Sunday-portioned part of it.

Lean Not on Your Own Understanding

Any doubters here? Even with only a grain of salt-sized humility, every one of us knows we seldom have the answers. Even when we think we do, our conclusions are often incomplete, misguided, and difficult to implement.

For two decades, I saw my role in business as being to read, study, analyze, and share information—through books, keynotes, coaching, and advising—about how today's great companies did what they did so well. Over the years, many clients told me, "I don't care what so-and-so business guru thinks; I'm paying you for what YOU think!" Needless to say, it was easy to stroll into a "lean-on-my-own-understanding," self-inflated ego trip. I fought this for years, yet I must admit that my flesh enjoyed being so highly regarded by others for my... *ahem*... obvious intellectual strengths! (I have repented. No worries.)

Even with all these books and speeches and with everyone else thinking I had it all together, down deep, I knew I did not. My hope was that no one could see through my façade to find how hopelessly little I did know, for that would have ruined *my* business.

Just like me, you will never understand everything you need to in order to grow your business toward the eternal impact God desires for you to make. We often need to be reminded of this, especially for those of us with many people under us in the organizational chart.

In *All* Your Ways Acknowledge Him

What does *all* mean?

It means... ALL!

All means all. Not part. Not some. Not just opening a meeting in prayer. Not just praying for more increase. Not just calling on Him in times of trouble, financial crisis, or employee injury.

All... means all.

All.

Why do I repeat the obvious? Sometimes, the obvious ain't. We know we *should* trust the Lord with ALL. I have found this easier to do in my family, my marriage, and with my kids... even with serving my faith community.

But I admit that, over the years, I struggled with *all* in my business. Yes, I began with my journey to align my business and my faith by praying for a couple of verses that encapsulated my convictions and values. (This is a great place to start, but it is only a start.)

When anyone asked me about my company's core convictions, I referred to these verses as my foundation. I was pleasantly surprised by the very positive response… even from nonbelievers. It was a small step toward unleashing and one that gave me confidence to continue the journey toward acknowledging Him in *all* my business ways.

He Shall Direct Our Paths

The word, *shall,* is defined as something that is expected to happen in the future. The Lord did not say…

- He might
- When He has time
- When you've made His *good list*
- Only when it gets too tough for you to handle
- After He thinks about it
- When He feels like it
- After you reach a certain level of spiritual maturity

Say this aloud: "HE SHALL DIRECT MY PATHS!"
Say it again.
Come on. No one is around you now. Say it AGAIN!
Directing your paths… the ultimate payback!
You must trust what you hear through your inner knowing and not doubt.

4.5. ARMOR UP

"Finally, my brethren, be strong in the Lord and in the power of His might. Put on the whole armor of God, that you may be able to stand against the wiles of the devil. For we do not wrestle against flesh and blood, but against principalities, against powers, against the rulers of the darkness of this age, against spiritual hosts of wickedness in the heavenly places. Therefore take up the whole armor of God, that you may be able to withstand in the evil day, and having done all, to stand."

~Ephesians 6:10-13

Satan is the prince of this world. He has primary control over the mechanisms of business. So as you employ your unfair advantage, the enemy will come after you! Count on it.

In Kyle Winker's fascinating book, *Silence Satan: Shutting Down the Enemy's Attacks, Threats, Lies, and Accusations*, he states,

> *"The weapons we're given as a part of Christ's uniform help us with our thinking. Satan barges into our lives with arguments as to why God can't use us, why we'll never be healed, or why our particular sins are too big to be forgiven. These are the doubts and discouragements he uses as obstacles to keep us from a life of victory."*[1]

The same things can be said about our business lives. As you begin to leverage your unfair advantage in your marketplace, the enemy will throw everything he has at you and your team.

Within Paul's description of the armor, I want you to focus on three significant thoughts:

1: Whole Armor

Partial armor is useless. Imagine a soldier entering battle without his helmet, backpack, boots, or weapon. Likewise, imagine a 2%er entering the battlefield of the marketplace that is controlled by the enemy without the full armor attached and ready for every enemy attack.

The six pieces of the full armor are the...

- **Belt of Truth** – The Word and upon other weapons are attached
- **Breastplate of Righteous** – To protect the heart and soul and to serve as a shining symbol to the enemy of your protection
- **Helmet of Salvation** – To protect the mind, the ears, and the thoughts
- **Shoes of the Gospel of Peace** – Footwear ready to stand firmly and not lose ground
- **Shield of Faith** – To block the fiery darts of the enemy and to protect the entire body from attacks
- **Sword of the Spirit** – The Word of God, the only attack weapon

Paul's admonition is to put on the *whole* armor, not just a piece or two. Without the full protective gear, you would be vulnerable for the enemy to slide into attack mode at your weakest point, his typical tactic.

Realize that five of the pieces are protective gear; only one is an attack weapon. If this is a potential spiritual war on you and your business, why are you limited to only one attack weapon? Read on.

2: Stand

Four times in Paul's description of the whole armor (Ephesians 6:10-20), he states that we should stand, not fight. That is fascinating to me, for why should we armor up and not fight?

Winkler offers magnificent insight into why Paul teaches us to take a stand. He teaches that the purpose of putting on the whole armor is…

> "…to find strength in the Lord's power so that you may stand. He (Paul) doesn't say to put on the armor in order to fight, but that in the Lord you may maintain the standing of your identity in Christ against the evil forces that seek to destroy you."[2]

As you armor up, realize that you are not seeking to march into battle as much as you are cloaking yourself in the power of the Lord to withstand (there it is again… stand) the wiles and deception of the enemy.

3: Wiles

In the Garden of Eden, the enemy floated subtle lies and deception to deceive Eve and Adam (Genesis 3). He attempted the same thing with Jesus during his 40 days of temptation (Matthew 4). The enemy's tactics have not changed in 6,000 years. He will do the same with you.

He will bring thoughts and ideas to you that could include…

- "You can't do this."
- "You don't have the team or the resources."
- "This is the craziest thing you've ever tried."
- "It will ruin your business."
- "Nobody will go along with you."
- "Have you lost your mind?"
- "What will your competitors think?"
- "You'll lose a ton of money and even your business."
- "No one will follow you."

- "You're not a strong enough leader to pull this off."
- "Are you really sure this is from God? Are you sure?"
- "You're not serious about this... Are you?"
- "You're just reading this crazy business book and are making the mistake of being expert-led like the fool says."

You get the drift.

And many of these are the light artillery compared to the bombs you could experience.

You will not always be attacked, but when you begin to be Spirit-led, you need to be fully armored-up.

This is why it's critically important as you prepare to unleash your unfair competitive advantage to put on the full, whole armor daily so you can take a stand through Christ's strength, not your own.

It's like the old story we've all heard in church about the elderly lady who sees the devil knocking on her door. She then calmly turns around says out loud, "Jesus, that's for you!"

One More Thing: The Enemy Must Flee

"Therefore submit to God. Resist the devil and he will flee from you."
~James 4:7

When you command the enemy to leave your business in the name of Jesus, he must comply! He has no choice!

Period!

None!

Therefore,

- Do not fight the devil on his turf. Remind him he has already been defeated, resist him, and he *must* flee; he has no choice!
- Do not fight a spiritual war with your mental ability. Fight it with the Word, just like Jesus (Matthew 4:1-11).
- Do not let the thought of the enemy coming after you frighten you, "for He who is in you is greater than he who is in the world" (1 John 4:4).
- Do not let the enemy linger around you or your team. Command him to leave, and he will leave!

In summary, remember...

- It's more than prayer.
- It's more than a voice.
- Be wholehearted.
- Trust in the Lord.
- Armor-up every day.

Once you embrace these five steps of preparation, you are ready to move on to unleashing the power of the Holy Spirit in your business.

Do not casually read or skip these steps. Bury them deep into your heart and soul before you launch into your competitive advantage. In so doing, you will give yourself a solid foundation for the Holy Spirit to manifest His presence through your business!

---

[1] Kyle Winkler, *Silence Satan: Shutting Down the Enemy's Attacks, Threats, Lies, and Accusations* (Lake Mary, FL: Passio, 2014), 150.

[2] Ibid., 142.

Belt of truth
Breastplate of righteousness
shoes / peace
shield / faith
sword / spirit
Helmet of salvation
STAND

CHAPTER 5

UNLEASH YOUR UNFAIR ADVANTAGE

"But you shall receive power when the Holy Spirit has come upon you."
~Acts 1:8a

Y ou've decided to make the big shift.

You know the potential roadblocks.

You've prepared yourself for what lies ahead.

Now, you are ready!

This section will guide you through six keys to unleashing your unfair advantage. I recommend you apply these in order, for they naturally build upon one another into a powerful culmination.

Here is how I suggest you attack this section.

First, read through all six without making notes. Get a sense for the flow, the content, and the momentum they produce.

Then, read each section one-at-a-time, and complete the short exercises in each section. I recommend you concentrate on one section per day. Trying to breeze through these in one sitting may limit the Spirit's ability to massage His words deep into your spirit.

Once you've implemented these six keys, you'll be ready to move on to Chapter 6, "Keep It Going."

Here ya go... what you've been waiting so patiently to learn.

5.1. PRACTICE

Practice (v): to do something again and again in order to become better at it; to do (something) regularly or constantly as an ordinary part of your life.

This definition of practice is exactly what you should desire to apply, allowing the power of the Holy Spirit to be an expected and everyday part of your business life.

Anyone who has played competitive sports understands the absolute necessity of practice. Professional shortstops and second basemen practice making double plays until they can do it in their sleep. Professional basketball players practice three-point shots until they can no longer lift their arms. Professional golfers hit dozens of buckets of golf balls until they can hit shots to exact yardage, time and time again.

In business, professional training and development programs inject a lot of practice before dismissing the employees to execute the training on the job. Professional service companies invest large amounts of practice time in how they handle customer calls before service reps take their first real customer call. Professional sales trainers conduct relentless mock interviews to teach salespeople how to listen to and close potential clients.

Imagine a newly-hired airline pilot being told on his first day, "Welcome to our flight team. Now, get over to Gate A12. Your first flight takes off in 30 minutes!"

In my book, *The Impacter: A Parable on Transformational Leadership*, I teach that confidence comes from competence. Once I practice and learn the fundamentals and intricacies of my role, my confidence expands exponentially. So in the bottom of the ninth inning, with the game on the line, I am confident and at ease to turn that double play, shoot the game-winning three-point shot, make the 20-foot birdie putt to win *The Masters,* or land the plane in a mighty storm... because I've practiced it a thousand times.

The exact same thing is true as we look to unleash the power of the Holy Spirit in our businesses.

Here are three steps to integrate into your practice: Identify the Witness, Start Small, and Fine Tune.

Identify the Witness

Your pastor or teacher shares a powerful truth, and something on your insides says to you, "Yeah! That's good! That's right!" You may even say it out loud as I do!

When the Holy Spirit hears the truth, He confirms it. And when He confirms it, your spirit senses it.

That's your internal witness.

The same Spirit that bears witness to you in a church service is available to do the same just thing through you at your workplace.

It's imperative to become more and more aware of His witness, even if you are already fully in touch with the Holy Spirit.

We can never over-practice this too much!

Reflect on the times at work when your witness—that inner knowing—was at total peace. Was it when you...

- Launched a big project?
- Hired a terrific person?
- Changed subcontractors?
- Cancelled a trip?
- Purchased a large piece of equipment?
- Signed that contract?
- Challenged an employee to step it up and work to his potential?
- Signed a contract with an advisor or coach?

Then, there are times when you can look back and say, "I *knew* I should *not* have"…

- Launched that big project!
- Hired that person!
- Changed subcontractors!
- Cancelled that trip!
- Purchased that piece of equipment!
- Signed that contract!
- Challenged that employee to step it up!
- Signed with that advisor or coach!

In both cases, it is highly likely that the Holy Spirit was already at work inside you, exhorting you to the make the right moves and reining you in from making the wrong ones.

It takes a conscientious and intentional effort to perpetually identify the witness. If you do not, you quickly will fall back into being world-led.

The more your practice, the easier it will become to identify the witness.

Start Small

"Give us this day our daily bread."
~Matthew 6:11

When I first learned this concept of *practice*, I did begin small. One particular experience really stands out.

On a recent driving business trip to meet with a retainer client in Atlanta, I quickly was approaching the huge, always busy I-285 bypass, which is filled with very fast and often crazy drivers. (Hey, it's the truth.)

Perhaps—like many of you—when I drive, I occasionally need to stop and… well… recycle some coffee! I also hate the idea of having to exit off and get back onto the incredibly busy and confusing exits of I-285.

So I decided to practice identifying the witness. I asked the Holy Spirit which of the next two exits, before hitting I-285, would be best for me!

On this trip, I was by myself, so without my wonderful wife along, I did not sense an obligation to make an extended Cracker Barrel stop. The Holy Spirit knows I would prefer a McDonald's on the same side of the interstate from which I exit.

Why a McDonald's? Confession: most McDonald's have a side door close to the rest rooms where you can sneak in, recycle, and sneak out without management seeing you. Normally, I do buy something—really, I do—but this time, I was in a little bit of a hurry. (Okay... I'll go to the prayer altar on Sunday and repent!)

As I approached the first exit, I did not sense a witness. Nothing. So I continued on, placing my trust in the Spirit and the second exit.

I slowed down, turned on my blinker, and eased onto the exit. I sensed something good here.

Then, what to my wondrous, big brown eyes did appear... but a McDonald's... on the same side of the interstate... and it had a SIDE DOOR!

"Yeah!" I shouted in the car! You would have, too, not only for the convenient recycling opportunity but also for the confirmation of the witness of the Spirit.

This small example was one of the first times I intentionally tuned into the Holy Spirit for a purely non-church or prayer-related activity. This witness was for a bathroom break on a business trip for heaven's sake (and my bladder's sake, too).

You, too, can start small with inviting the Holy Spirit into your business by asking "should I" questions such as...

- "Should I meet with this person today or at another time?"

- "Should I attend this meeting?"
- "Should I call this customer?"
- "Should I go to lunch here or there?"
- "Should I write that letter or email now or later today?"
- "Should I come in early tomorrow or stay late tonight to finish this project?"

There are dozens more we could add to this basic list, but you get the idea. The possibilities to start small are endless.

I encourage you to start with small, low-risk opportunities to practice and gain confidence in identifying the witness inside you. Trust me… He will enjoy you intentionally seeking Him and will make Himself more and more known to you as you practice.

Fine-Tune

You are surrounded by a lot of spiritual noise. The enemy is speaking to you all the time, bombarding you with unrelenting noise and messages from the world he controls.

But through His Holy Spirit, God also is speaking to you all the time. Without intentional practice, it would be so easy for God's voice to be drowned out by the enemies. It is therefore critical that you fine-tune your Holy-Spirit-receiving mechanisms to pick up His channel.

As we previously discussed, a great analogy is to think of a fine-tuning mechanism like a radio receiver. If the Holy Spirit is speaking to you on FM, you need to be listening on the FM band, not the AM band. Now, you really may like the AM band, but if the Holy Spirit prefers FM, that is where you need to be.

If He is speaking on the FM band, regardless of the size and power of your AM receiver and speakers, you'll never be able to hear Him.

Therefore, the more you practice tuning in on His FM band, and the more you adjust your tuning mechanisms, the more clearly and powerfully you will hear His leadings.

As you begin, you will experience some successes ("next exit") and some failures. I'd like to share two stories with the desire to teach you from my personal experience. One was a big failure, and the other was a big success.

First, let me share the big success.

You are holding it in your hands!

Although I was two-thirds finished with writing the follow-up book in *The Impacter* series, I hit a barrier. At first, I was not sure if the barrier was self-imposed or Spirit-ordained.

I quickly discerned it was the witness of the Spirit and not of my flesh.

One morning, while asking the Holy Spirit what I was to do, He said to me (not in an audible voice but in that inner knowing), "Write a book on how to involve me more powerfully in the businesses of believers."

I immediately set aside the book I was writing and immediately began seeking His words for *Our Unfair Advantage*.

As I pen this manuscript under the guidance of the Holy Spirit, it is without question the most-anticipated book ever of my 14 previous books!

Without question, this has been the most fulfilling, fun, and potentially, most important work of my life.

Only through previous practice was I certain this was indeed the Spirit. And I immediately obeyed.

Now for the big fail.

A few years ago, my wife and I were visiting our son at his Christian boys' school in Southern Missouri. On the last day of this visit, I wore one of my prized possessions: a brand new University of Louisville National Championship men's basketball polo shirt given to me as a gift by my sister and brother. Having grown up in a small town just south of Louisville and having played basketball all though high school, I am a huge UL men's basketball fan. I even have a basketball signed by Denny Crum proudly displayed in its glass container on my desk!

UL fans had waited 18 years for another national championship, so this shirt was especially fun to wear.

Just minutes before we were to leave, one of our son's friends came up to us, and we began to chat. This tall, skinny 17-year-old boy jumped in excitement in seeing my shirt. He was from Louisville and, like me, was a huge UL fan. We talked about the players, the championship, and how happy we were to be reining national champs.

Then, I heard a voice inside me—not an audible voice but a voice as loud and clear—say to me, "Give him your shirt!"

My first response was, "Get behind me, Satan!" (Hey, that would have been yours, too, I bet!)

I remember thinking, "This surely can't be the voice of the Lord. Why would He want me to give up my new favorite shirt to a kid I don't even know?"

You already know where this is going, don't you!

As the boy walked away, I again heard, "Give him the shirt. You have lots of clean shirts in the trunk of your car."

The truth is I hesitated, said goodbye to our son, and drove off… still wearing the prized shirt.

In less than five minutes, I turned to Brenda and told her what had happened. She quickly agreed with the Holy Spirit that I should have given the shirt to the boy.

Yet instead of turning around, I drove 1.5 days back to Pensacola, washed the shirt, and mailed it to the boy with a note saying that my delayed obedience was actually disobedience. I repented for my disobedience, asked and received forgiveness, and prayed the shirt would bless the boy.

My son told me later that the boy loved the shirt so much he did not want to take it off to wash it.

For me, this was a resounding, "I-*knew*-I-should-have-given-the-shirt-to-him" experience. Like you, we all have had many of these in our careers.

But that is about to change!

In my failure, I learned many valuable lessons, including...

- How to recognize the distinct and powerful inner knowing of the Holy Spirit
- To act immediately lest you be in disobedience
- To encounter the blessing of immediate obedience rather than the heaviness of delayed obedience

Identify your witness. Start small. Then, fine tune.

It takes practice. Intentional practice. In time, your practice will strengthen your spiritual fine-tuning receiver to be always clearly receiving the broadcasts of the Holy Spirit.

Here is an action plan to help you get started with your practice.

Practice Action Plan

List five small ways you can begin to practice. What are some decisions at work in which you can seek the Holy Spirit's guidance with minimal downside (e.g. where to eat lunch, what project action to take next, who needs your help, etc.). Record what you learn.

Decision #1: _____

How did you tune in?

What got in your way of tuning in?

What did you learn?

Decision #2: _____

How did you tune in?

What got in your way of tuning in?

What did you learn?

Decision #3: _____

How did you tune in?

What got in your way of tuning in?

What did you learn?

Decision #4: _____

How did you tune in?

What got in your way of tuning in?

What did you learn?

Decision #5: _____

How did you tune in?

What got in your way of tuning in?

What did you learn?

5.2. CHECK BEFORE YOU ACT

Check (n): a sudden stoppage of a forward course or progress; a sudden pause or break in a progression; the act of testing or verifying

How people make decisions has always fascinated me. What influences people to make the decisions they do? How do persuasive messages and environmental factors impact decision-making?

Throughout my master's and doctoral studies, I focused on the interpersonal and psychological variables in small groups' decision-making. I invested years of in-depth study and research on such topics as…

- Consensus seeking and compromise
- Leadership styles and the use of power in groups
- Non-verbal communication dynamics
- Interracial and cross-cultural communication
- Group Think
- The rhetoric of Aristotle, including the effects of ethos, pathos, and logos
- The power of deductive, inductive, and analogous reasoning
- The impact of communication apprehension in the decision-making process in male and female problem-solving dyads

Believe it or not, that last one was the focus of both my master's thesis and my Ph.D. dissertation. Great reads for insomnia!

With so many years of devoted study, learning from some the greatest academic minds in the world and from multiple professional publications, I now look back with one overriding conclusion...

Man, oh Man, did I get it all wrong!

Over the last 20 years, I have researched how the greatest leader and decision-maker of all time, Jesus, made decisions.

Did the greatest leader and business mind of all time ever...

- Seek consensus or majority vote from his disciples?
- Reflect on the works of Socrates, Aristotle, or Plato?
- Think deeply on the interpersonal dynamics of his words?
- Form customer focus groups to uncover trends and preferences?
- Seek high-priced experts for their wisdom?

Man, oh Man, did I get it all wrong!

No, Jesus had an entirely new, innovative, and unheard-of decision-making process.

He always, in every situation, checked with the Spirit of God before he acted.

"Then Jesus answered and said to them, 'Most assuredly, I say to you, the Son can do nothing of Himself, but what He sees the Father do; for whatever He does, the Son also does in like manner. For the Father loves the Son, and shows Him all things that He Himself does; and He will show Him greater works than these, that you may marvel.'" (John 5:19-20)

Jesus checked with the Spirit of God the Father, the Holy Spirit!

> *"For I have not spoken on My own authority; but the Father who sent Me gave Me a command, what I should say and what I should speak. And I know that His command is everlasting life. Therefore, whatever I speak, just as the Father has told Me, so I speak."*
> (John 12:49-50)

> *"Do you not believe that I am in the Father, and the Father in Me? The words that I speak to you I do not speak on My own authority; but the Father who dwells in Me does the works." (John 14:10)*

Jesus always checked on the inside before He did or said anything.

Here are three simple ways to help train yourself in how to check before you act: slow down, block the outside, and make one final check.

Slow Down

Ever heard any of these?

- "It's the fast that eat the slow."
- "Move fast or die."
- "This is urgent."
- "I need this done yesterday."
- "Speed it up; don't slow us down."
- "They just don't work fast enough."
- "We haven't got all day."
- "Gotta get on with it!"
- "Come on! Come on! Come on!"

- "Just ship it!"

In our business world, we are bombarded every day and every hour with seemingly critical tasks or decision that *must* be completed *now*. We easily can reconcile ourselves to the false belief of, "Well, that's just business."

Too many times, I have fallen into this same trap. When I ran a small, semi-custom, home-building company, the pressure to get another draw to pay my carpentry crew forced me to jump from house-to-house to complete the quickest stage to get the fastest bank draw. The owner of the company never understood why I was jumping around in what seemed to be a random, helter-skelter order.

Looking back, I was money-led totally in the way I operated as I sold out to getting the dollar as quickly as I could. But because I had a payroll to meet (including mine) and subcontractors to pay, I did not know any other way.

I wish now that someone had taught me to slow down, just like Jesus.

> "Then the scribes and Pharisees brought to Him a woman caught in adultery. And when they had set her in the midst, they said to Him, 'Teacher, this woman was caught in adultery, in the very act. Now Moses, in the law, commanded us that such should be stoned. But what do You say?' This they said, testing Him, that they might have something of which to accuse Him. But Jesus stooped down and wrote on the ground with His finger, as though He did not hear. So when they continued asking Him, He raised Himself up and said to them, 'He who is without sin among you, let him throw a stone at her first.' And again He stooped down and wrote on the ground. Then those who heard it, being convicted by their conscience, went out one by one, beginning with

*the oldest even to the last. And Jesus was left alone, and
the woman standing in the midst." (John 8:3-9)*

Here's the setting. Religious leaders barged into the temple
courts where Jesus was teaching a large crowd, cruelly embar-
rassed a woman in public, and demanded in front of everyone
that Jesus give them an immediate answer to their questions.

Everyone could see these men were dead serious, literally,
as they carried stones in their hands, threatening to kill the
woman or possibly Jesus himself.

They forced Jesus into an either-or dilemma: Kill her as the
Law teaches or set her free and break the Law.

So how did Jesus react to this life-threatening situation?

He knelt down on his knees and wrote in the dirt... and said
nothing!

Now *that* infuriated the men even more. You can sense their
unrighteous indignation when they again demanded Jesus answer their question: "What say you? Kill her or set her free?
Option A or Option B? Answer us... NOW!"

So how did Jesus react to this second and even more intense
life-threatening situation?

He continued to write in the dirt.

When and only when Jesus was fully ready to answer, he
stood up and stated, "I say Option C... Go ahead and kill her if
you have never sinned yourself." He then knelt back down and
continued to write in the dirt.

So what was Jesus doing when he first knelt down? Why did
he do this? What was he doing?

I believe he slowed down to ask God's Holy Spirit living inside him, "Spirit, what do you want me to say and do?"

I believe he did exactly what the Spirit instructed him to do.
His instructions may have included, "Just pause here for effect.
Let's make them all feel this a little more intensely."

There is no earthly, rational way to have come up with his response. It was supernatural. Only the Holy Spirit could have given this response to him.

The only logical explanation to his amazing, out-of-this-world answer is that it indeed came from an amazing, out-of-this-world Spirit.

Just as Jesus slowed down to check his spirit in a life threatening circumstance, you can slow down and check your spirit in any business situation you face.

Block the Outside

The men surrounding Jesus demanded an answer and demanded it now. Their pressure was from the outside.

If Jesus had allowed the pressures of the situation to lead him, he could have made a terrible—but quick—decision. Instead, he chose to be led from the inside where the Spirit reigns.

No need to raise your hands or talk yourself down. We have all succumbed to outside pressures to do something, including...

- Signing a contract on the deadline date
- Hiring a person to fill an open slot rather than to grow the business
- Giving away far too much profit just to close a deal
- Making a knee-jerk decision in a meeting only because others expected it of you
- Agreeing to attend that banquet or luncheon when you did not have the desire, time, or funds
- Throwing together a sloppy proposal because the prospect expected it immediately

These are just a few of the decisions I have reached over the years without checking on the inside. If you've done any of these, too, then you have the foundation to write your own book!

You may be asking, "So, Jim, are you telling us to ignore everything on the outside and only check on the inside before making a business decision?" No, I am not suggesting that at all.

God gave a mind to all of us with the ability to read, research, analyze, reflect, seek facts, assess, and probe. He expects us to use our intellect to the best of our abilities to understand all we can.

But when you've done all you can do, before you make the final decision and act, listen again from the inside where the Spirit dwells.

Remember, the Holy Spirit prompts you from the inside. The enemy tries to pressure you from the outside!

Your inside must always override the outside voices with your inside Spirit.

> Remember, the Holy Spirit prompts you from the inside. The enemy tries to pressure you from the outside!

Final Check

The *final check* is often a quick verification for yourself, your spirit that bears witness with the Holy Spirit inside you. By no means is this an attempt to delay or postpone action but a simple exhortation to take the time for one final check on the inside.

In my business, I fly all over the country and, sometimes, internationally. I often have noticed one of the pilots slowly inspecting the fuselage, wings, and landing gear of the plane before takeoff. It is reassuring to me, their "valued customer," that the leader is taking the time to make one final check of all the systems.

Even if the flight leaves a few minutes late due to the pilot's safety check, do you think I get upset? No way. I am thrilled the crew thought enough of their profession to ensure, as best as they could, the safe operation of the plane.

I recommend to my coaching clients that, before they make that next important decision, to set aside all their data, reports, paperwork, and notes and get away to a quiet place to ask the Spirit what to do.

So often, this final check removes you from the pressure-packed environment, reassures you of the best decision, and builds more confidence and clarity in your spirit about the goodness of the decision. Then, you can go ahead and act with a sense of peace concerning the decision.

Check Before You Act Action Plan

The second key to unleashing the power of the Holy Spirit in your business is to *check before you act*, so...

- Slow down.
- Block the outside.
- Take a final check.

List 3-5 short-term decisions you need to make. Then, assess them one at a time.

Decision #1: _____

How did you slow down?

How did you block the outside?

What did the final check confirm?

Decision #2: _____

How did you slow down?

How did you block the outside?

What did the final check confirm?

Decision #3: _____

How did you slow down?

How did you block the outside?

What did the final check confirm?

Decision #4: _____

How did you slow down?

How did you block the outside?

What did the final check confirm?

Decision #5: _____

How did you slow down?

How did you block the outside?

What did the final check confirm?

5.3. SEEK A WITNESS

Witness (n): attestation of a fact or event; one who has personal knowledge of something

Countless criminal cases in America have been decided based on the testimony of just one witness, someone who was at the crime scene and knows what happened. Through their witness, they are able confirm the truth of their experience. Regardless of the opposing evidence, the testimony of one witness easily can override the voices of dozens of non-witness experts.

The same is true with your Spirit, your one, all-powerful, all-knowing, and internal witness.

The third key to unleashing the power of the Holy Spirit in your business is to *seek a witness* in all you do.

The True Witness

"A faithful witness does not lie. But a false witness will utter lies."
~*Proverbs 14:5*

Have you ever had someone lie to you at work? An employee? A boss? A vendor? A customer? Of course you have. If you've been in business for more than 24 hours, someone likely has told you a little fib or a big, fat, juicy lie.

But how did you know it was a lie? What told you that this person was not being truthful? What was it that helped you see through the lie?

The answer is simple. You already knew the truth!

Whether it was a set of numbers, a history of the transaction, a missing element of a report, or even another person, something inside you already had a sense of the truth. It was easy to recognize an imposter.

In many cases, it was the Spirit, the true Witness living inside you that confirmed the truth or the falsehood.

Sometimes, though, we all get fooled. We hear something and think, "Gee, I don't know. That sounds goods. It's reasonable. I guess it could be that way. I'm not sure, and I would hate to accuse them of something and be wrong."

When are we fooled? When we fall back into old habits of being head-led or idea-led or feelings-led rather than being Spirit-led.

So how can you distinguish between the true witness and the false witness?

The true witness gives you…

- Peace (Philippians 4:7)
- Unity (Ephesians 4:3)
- Patience (Galatians 5:5)
- Strength (Ephesians 3:16)
- Insight (1 Corinthians 2:10, 13)
- Joy (1 Thessalonians 1:6)
- Comfort (Acts 9:31)
- Fruit (Galatians 5:22-23)

The false witness causes you…

- Turmoil
- Discomfort
- Anxiety
- Weakness
- Confusion
- Fear
- Uncertainty
- Stress

As you seek a witness on a decision, keep these lists handy to remind yourself how to distinguish quickly between the true witness and the false witness.

Remember, the Spirit will guide you into all truth (John 16:13). So, in reality, you only need to seek one witness, the true witness of the Holy Spirit.

One Witness Is Enough

"The Spirit Himself bears witness with our spirit that we are children of God."

~Romans 8:16

A common business colloquialism is, "It's lonely at the top."

Every day, you make dozens of decisions about what to work on, avoid, finish, or delay. The higher you are in the company, the more often you make decisions with potentially huge ramifications. The bigger the decisions, the fewer number of people you are at liberty to involve in the decision.

Sometimes, it is indeed lonely in business.

And it is never lonelier when you stand all alone on an issue.

Whether you are at the top or the bottom of the company's chain-of-command, you face times and decisions in which you are the only person on one side of an issue. In these times, you look for someone to rally to your side, to come to your rescue, and to reassure you of your position.

This is the perfect time to seek the one true witness, for He is enough.

It's just like a stoplight. Red means *stop...* now. Yellow means *proceed with caution*. More specifically, it means *slow down*.

Green means *go*.

In my experience, the Spirit sometimes gives a red light, sometimes a yellow, and sometimes a green.

So here is one way to seek a witness. If you sense...

- **Anxiety or uncertainty** – Stop! It's likely a red light.
- **Nothing** – Wait and keep seeking. It's likely a yellow light.
- **Peace and power** – Go and GO NOW! You've got a Holy Spirit green light to put the pedal to the metal!

Two Witnesses Are Even Better

"It seemed good to us, being assembled with one accord, to send chosen men to you with our beloved Barnabas and Paul."

~Acts 15:25

"For it seemed good to the Holy Spirit, and to us, to lay upon you no greater burden than these necessary things."

~Acts 15:28

"However, it seemed good to Silas to remain there."

~Acts 15:34

Strong's Dictionary defines witness as "to testify jointly, i.e. corroborate by (concurrent) evidence; testify unto; bear joint witness." In each of these verses above, believers came together as co-witnesses on the same decision. "It seemed good to the Holy Spirit and to us" is a perfect example of the co-witness. The Holy Spirit said to them individually, "Yes, that's a good decision," and then together they jointly corroborated their internal witnesses.

Although your solo witness with the Holy Spirit certainly is enough, a witness of two or more believers is even better!

Here is an example of the power of the two-person co-witnesses.

Recently, I addressed a large group of Christian business leaders as the closing keynote in a regional conference. I shared a quick overview of the principles in this book. During the message, I sensed the Holy Spirit prompting me to camp out on seeking a co-witness.

Three days after the conference, I received a long and detailed e-mail from one of the attendees, a business icon in this state and a founding member of this prestigious Christian business organization for that region.

After a quick overview of the problem, he wrote in his e-mail,

> *"Bottom line, I'm driving home last night and remembered your message. I turned off the radio, verbally asked the Holy Spirit what I should do in this situation. I felt impressed to call my assistant office manager and ask her for her thoughts on the matter (she's a GREAT gal, loves the Lord, but I have NEVER done this!)"*

My friend went on to describe how, together, they had a powerful and fast co-witness with a great solution. He concluded his e-mail by saying,

> *"(Needless to say) I would NEVER have come up with this solution on my own. I don't know how many other people at that meeting had such IMMEDIATE application of the principles you taught but I sure did and I appreciate you being obedient to the Lord and making the effort to speak to our group!"*

This is an absolutely perfect example of seeking a co-witness. You can sense the confidence and joy in his words as well as the implied confidence that he would keep seeking both the witness and the co-witness in his business.

When you have a powerful at-work team of co-witnesses, just like the disciples did in the Upper Room, you can overcome anything in your business world.

However, a co-witness is not always so easy or fast. The stickiest of situations is when you ask a colleague or friend for a co-witness, but you are on different sides of the issue. What should you do then?

My social media and website strategy coach is a wonderful, Spirit-filled believer and a best-selling author. He knows my business as well or better than me. He continues to coach and guide all my digital marketing and positioning efforts.

Naturally, I ask him on many occasions, "Here is what I am thinking. Have you got a witness on this?"

Often, he immediately confirms what I am sensing. Sometimes, he does not.

Now, what should I do?

Because he has such intimate knowledge of my platform, my goals, and how God has called me to fill a slot in His perfect plan, I go back again to seek my witness on the decision.

Going deeper with the Spirit only draws me into a closer, more powerful relationship. Often, it only takes a short while, from minutes to a few days, for the decision to be settled in my Spirit.

In the end, the decision is mine. I do what I am led to do. And the extra time with the Lord gives me additional strength, peace, and commitment.

The funny thing is that, after I implement my decision, my media guru friend often says, "Now I can see more clearly why you chose that option. I had not thought of it from that perspective. I know it will work for you."

In the end, I get the co-witness I initially sought. I just had to step out in faith in response to my witness.

The Greatest Team-Building Strategy

"Hey, Tom, can I ask you for your help? I am about to make a big decision on… I want to be sure I am hearing from the Lord exactly what He wants me to do. Here is what I sense He is telling me… Do you have a witness on this?"

Imagine the reaction of Tom, another 2%er in your company.

Imagine how humbled and overwhelmed he would feel to even be asked to help you on such an important question.

If Tom knows the power of the co-witness, he'll know what to do.

Just think about the many team-building strengths of inviting others to be your co-witnesses at work. Seeking a co-witness with your colleagues…

- Builds trust in your decisions
- Solidifies the Biblical foundation of your business
- Demonstrates your willingness to listen to your team's heart and spirit
- Grows spiritual muscle and discernment throughout your company
- Reminds others to do the same concerning their decisions
- Reassures others even in decisions on which they do not agree

This is the most powerful team-building question ever: "DO YOU HAVE A WITNESS?"

Seek a Witness Action Plan

Here is a simple, four-question, *Seek a Witness* Action Plan. Answer these in order.

Decision #1 _____

Do I have a personal witness about this decision or action?

Do I need a co-witness on this?

If so, who should I ask for a co-witness?

Does he/she have a witness about this?

My witness decision is:

Decision #2 _____

Do I have a personal witness about this decision or action?

Do I need a co-witness on this?

If so, who should I ask for a co-witness?

Does he/she have a witness about this?

My witness decision is:

Decision #3 _____

Do I have a personal witness about this decision or action?

Do I need a co-witness on this?

If so, who should I ask for a co-witness?

Does he/she have a witness about this?

My witness decision is:

Decision #4 _____

Do I have a personal witness about this decision or action?

Do I need a co-witness on this?

If so, who should I ask for a co-witness?

Does he/she have a witness about this?

My witness decision is:

Decision #5 _____

Do I have a personal witness about this decision or action?

Do I need a co-witness on this?

If so, who should I ask for a co-witness?

Does he/she have a witness about this?

My witness decision is:

5.4. QUENCH NOT THE SPIRIT

Quench (v): put out; extinguish; to bring something to an end

I was a teenager during the Vietnam War. Every day for years during the nightly news programs, we heard that day's casualty count, the numbers of confirmed heroes who died for our freedom.

One of the most dramatic elements of the War was to learn of the many men being held as prisoners of war in what was caustically called the "Hanoi Hilton," a large compound where soldiers were mercilessly tortured for years.

For almost a decade, my good friend, Dr. Steve Linnville, has served on a phenomenal team of medical and psychological specialists who study the mental and physical effects of captivity on POWs from Vietnam, Desert Storm, and Operation Iraqi Freedom. Hundreds of these heroes, both men and women, frequently visit the Robert E. Mitchell Center on the Pensacola Naval Aviation Station for extensive physical evaluations and assessments.

A key question being asked in their longitudinal research is, "What are the key differences between soldiers who survived years of horrendous torture and soldiers who did not?"

Perhaps the most amazing finding of their research to date is this: *optimism* is the most important characteristic to predicting resiliency and the absence of any psychological disorder.

The greatest contributor to this resiliency is *faith*. For many, their faith was in God. For others, their faith was for a better future.

Why mention research findings on repatriated POWs in a book on how to unleash the Holy Spirit in business?

First, the Spirit led me to include this. Enough said!

Second, those who survived after facing minute upon minute, hour upon hour, day upon day, and year upon year of extreme physical and mental torture did so because they did not quench the spirit living inside them.

Yes, many of the Vietnam POWs are believers, and even the few stories I've heard about their inhumane treatment make my so-called personal and professional challenges pale into insignificance.

> "Rejoice always, pray without ceasing, in everything give thanks; for this is the will of God in Christ Jesus for you. Do not quench the Spirit."
> (1 Thessalonians 5:16-19)

Let's admit the truth: It's easy to quench the Spirit.

Sundays are the days we traditionally gather in our houses of worship, singing songs, thanking God for His Spirit, and sometimes hearing messages and Bible verses about the ways and wonders of the Holy Spirit.

We pray and say *amen* as we sense something churning on the inside, something good and something that causes us to reflect deeply on our personal spiritual walk with God.

After the service, we smile and shake hands with our friends, talk about the great message and music, joke about how we were "convicted," and make our way out the door and into our cars. No sooner than we've left the parking lot, we've left the teachings, the messages, the scriptures, and the promptings inside the building.

Again, we quench the Spirit of God.

We are too quick to say to ourselves, "That message was all about my personal walk anyway. What's that got to do with my business? Monday's just around the corner, and I've gotta get ready for the battle!"

Is it any wonder that so many of us rarely see the power of the Holy Spirit moving through our work or our colleagues?

It is so easy to leave the teachings, impressions, and exhortations from our spiritual leaders in the pews and hallways of a designated Sunday building.

For decades, we've all heard about the "Sunday-Monday divide" as harbingers of gloom wring their collective hands over the imagined demise of society and business without God.

The easiest way to bridge the great Sunday-Monday business divide is to refuse to allow yourself to quench the Holy Spirit in your work.

There are three ways in which we commonly quench the Spirit: ignoring Him, smothering Him, and grieving Him.

1. Ignoring Him

"Having eyes, do you not see? And having ears, do you not hear. And do you not remember?"

~Mark 8:18

Ignore means to refuse to show that you hear or see and to do nothing about or in response to something or someone. Perhaps the easiest way to quench the Spirit is to ignore Him.

The owner of a business I was advising instructed his lead salesmen to prepare a company-wide rollout plan on how to implement the leadership principles in my book, *The Impacter*, throughout their company. But I was only brought into the project at the end, after the plan had already been developed.

The author of the book was sitting in the room, willing and available to guide the process.

The author was "in the house" but basically was ignored.

So many business professionals I advise are guilty of ignoring the experts right in front of them. Even more so… the Expert living inside them!

The author of *The Book* lives in your house. He is willing and available anytime to guide you concerning how to integrate His perfect wisdom into your company.

Ignoring someone or something can be subtle or blatant. It can range from making a knee-jerk decision to never including Him in anything you do, think, or decide.

But you desire to be evermore led by the Spirit.

2. Smothering Him

Smother means to cover something in order to keep it from growing or spreading… to try to keep something from happening.

Sometimes, the answer seems obvious. It's obvious we need to…

- Invest in that equipment
- Attend that trade show
- Jump into that new advertising program
- Fire that employee
- Take charge of that problem

It is easy to be dominated by what appears to be obvious.

Remember Martha (Luke 10:40) as she frantically cooked a dinner and rudely interrupted Jesus' teaching in front of a house full of guests? What appeared obvious to Martha was not the most important thing.

She attempted to smother the Spirit working in and through people and was chastised gently. Everyone there, including Martha, learned it is far more important to focus on Him and not on the pressures of the day.

How are we most tempted to smother the Spirit? When…

- All the *facts* say one thing, but the Spirit says another

- All the *experts* say one thing, but the Spirit says another
- All your *staff* says one thing, but the Spirit says another
- You decide to move forward come hell or high water
- You stubbornly cling to the belief that failure is not an option
- You refuse to seek a co-witness
- You hear, "Give him your shirt," but you quickly put that our of your mind

But when you refuse to smother the Spirit in your business, the enemy loses on his own battlefield!

Be aware that the enemy loves nothing more than to push and prod you in an attempt to smother the move of the Spirit in your business.

But when you refuse to smother the Spirit in your business, the enemy loses on his own battlefield!

3. Grieving Him

"And do not grieve the Holy Spirit of God, by whom you were sealed for the day of redemption."

~Ephesians 4:30

Have you ever done something you knew was wrong, but you kept doing it anyway?

Eating a big bowl of ice cream every night? Playing golf or going fishing every Saturday while your spouse sits at home? Telling your kids over and over you are too tired to play with them now but to ask tomorrow?

Or, in your business, have you ever convinced yourself to…

- Hang onto an employee that should have left years ago?
- Put up with a top client's profanities or drunkenness on your expense account?
- Turn your head as your CFO cheats on his wife or blatantly breaks company protocol or policy?
- Allow a long-term customer's unwarranted rudeness to your employees?
- ...or any number of other things, all with the hope of helping the business?

Grieve means to cause someone to feel sad or unhappy... to cause him or her to suffer. Yes, you can grieve the Spirit through your business. You also can grieve Him through insults.

> *"Of how much worse punishment, do you suppose, will he be thought worthy who has trampled the Son of God underfoot, counted the blood of the covenant by which he was sanctified a common thing, and insulted the Spirit of grace." (Hebrews 10:29)*

One of the easiest ways I've learned to be more sensitive to how the Spirit is grieved is to be more aware of the times when I simply shake my head in disbelief because of another's actions.

When I am on top of my unleashing-the-power-of-the-Holy Spirit game, I ask myself, "Now, why did I just shake my head at that?"

In most cases, it is a reasonable reaction in response to someone cutting me off in traffic, standing oblivious to blocking the entire aisle with their cart, etc.

At work, you could find yourself shaking your head at things like...

- What some people say in meetings
- Leaders who are constantly late for their own meetings
- A person's or team's unwillingness to complete an assigned task
- Sloppy work
- Empty coffee pots left by the last person filling their cup

I intentionally ask myself whether these actions are grieving my flesh or grieving the Spirit inside me.

In many cases, it is just my flesh. For example, take the empty coffee pot. It is a struggle still, but I remind myself that my Savior came to serve and not to be served. Therefore, it is a blessing to others to clean out the grounds, pour clean water into the bin, and brew up a piping hot, fresh pot of coffee for me and others.

This is a simple but all-too-common example of how to transform a grievance of the flesh to be a blessing to others.

If it grieves my flesh, I fix it if I can and then forget about it.

If it grieves my spirit, I reflect on it some more to get to the core reason why I feel the way I do. I ask the Holy Spirit,

- "Why are you grieved over this?"
- "What do you desire me to do about it?"
- "How can I prevent this from happening in the future?"
- "What do you need me to learn about this?"
- "What do you desire me to tell others about this?"
- "Is this something I need to repent from?"

The last thing you need in your office is a grieving Spirit inside you or others.

A grieving Spirit is a direct indication that you or someone else around you is off-base and in need of a course correction.

Quench Not the Spirit Action Plan

Reflect on your current business problems, priorities, and pressures. In regard to the Holy Spirit, where have you recently…

Ignored Him –

Smothered Him –

Grieved Him –

Take 10 minutes now to lift these situations to the Lord and for Him to speak to you through His Spirit. Then, write below what the Spirit is instructing you to do. Give this action plan to an accountability partner (e.g. spouse, colleague, spiritual mentor, coach, etc.). Ask your accountability partner to seek a co-witness with you on these actions, to pray with you, and to hold you accountable for their implementation.

Action 1:

Action 2:

Action 3:

Action 4:

5.5. DON'T BE MOVED

Move (v): to start away from some point or place; to change position or posture

Get ready. Here comes the really hard part. This is the time when the enemy will be in full attack mode. Why?

- You've practiced.
- You've checked your Spirit before making the final decision.
- You've got a strong witness, either by yourself or with others.
- You have purposed in your heart not to quench the Spirit.

Now, the enemy will do everything in his power to fill you with doubts, uncertainty, and anxiety. He will pull out his full artillery and will viciously attack you when...

- All the numbers don't seem to add up
- Majority opinion is against you
- Competitors are fleeing while you are entering
- Success looks bleak at best
- Common sense says it's a dumb move
- Everyone is saying, "Don't do it!"

But you have the ultimate unfair advantage living inside you. By now, He already has confirmed in you that this decision is the Lord's will for your business. You know that you know that you know this decision is of the Lord.

The fastest, easiest, and most-effective way to see the power of the Holy Spirit in your business (and in your life) is to follow the instructions Mary gave to the servants just before Jesus turned the water into wine:

> "*His mother said to the servants, 'Whatever He says to you, do it.'*" (Luke 2:5)

Just do what He says!

Here are three powerful ways to not be moved: stay on focus, speak back, and stand firm.

1. Stay on Focus

"Brethren, I do not count myself to have apprehended; but one thing I do, forgetting those things which are behind and reaching forward to those things which are ahead, I press toward the goal for the prize of the upward call of God in Christ Jesus." (Philippians 3:13-14)

Many entrepreneurs today have what I call, "Squirrel Disease." If you are a typical entrepreneur, by design, your brain always is active, thinking, scheming, and dreaming with not enough attention to details or implementation minutia required for success. It's about the new idea, the new opportunity, the fresh approach, the huge potential, and the latest and greatest of whatever is now in front of you.

Being around you is like an open-topped kettle of popcorn, a non-stop flow of marketplace ADHD on steroids.

In my advising and coaching role, I help entrepreneurs and leaders clarify their goals and maximize their strengths while making their weaknesses irrelevant. Sometimes, it is an overwhelming and frustrating challenge with those afflicted by Squirrel Disease.

By their very nature, these wonderful, energetic, and intelligent men and woman desperately desire to succeed and do so for the glory of the Lord. Yet they are not naturally wired to stay on focus, so it is both a professional and a spiritual challenge to keep them accountable and on target.

I know it's a challenge for them. They know it's a challenge for them. The enemy also knows it's a challenge for them.

This is why it is so critical at this time to not be moved, for you know that this decision to act...

- Is of the Lord through the confirmation of the Holy Spirit
- Is what the Spirit wants you to do
- Is how the Spirit desires you to proceed

Although the challenge is great, you can stay on focus.

"Thus Noah did; according to all that God commanded him, so he did Noah on building the ark." (Genesis 6:20)

We know that Noah was 500 years old when first mentioned in the Bible (Genesis 5:32) and 600 years old when he entered the ark (Genesis 7:6). So construction of this floating city could have taken his family somewhere around 100 years or more.

Imagine...

- 100+ years of daily insults and ridicule from society as you labored in the Lord's work
- Nights, weeks, months, and perhaps years of frustration, weariness, and spiritual attacks on your body, mind, and soul
- Hoards of the enemy's imps exploiting lost souls to compound your efforts relentlessly to complete the task
- Focusing on one and only one goal for 100+ years

Just like Noah, once you decide, you must stay on focus. Yes, it can be done, and you can do it, too.

2. Speak Back

"For the word of God is living and powerful, and sharper than any two-edged sword, piercing even to the division of soul and spirit, and of joints and marrow, and is a discerner of the thoughts and intents of the heart." (Hebrews 4:12)

The Spirit drives you to succeed. The enemy desires that you fail.

One of the best ways to extinguish the fiery darts of the enemy is to speak back to him! Kyle Winkler writes in *Silence Satan,*

> *"I believe that when the Word of God is spoken through the mouths of those in Christ, it contains the same power as if God has spoken it Himself. The words must maintain the authority of God, otherwise they couldn't accomplish anything. These are His words, not ours, after all."*[1]

Winkler suggests there are three overriding benefits to speaking the Word of God directly to the enemy. First, speaking Scripture renews the mind. The spoken word is powerful, and "that same power that gave life to the universe will give new life to you."[2]

Second, it makes the enemy flee. Winkler writes, "The father of lies has no power when the truth of the Father is present."[3]

Third, speaking Scripture keeps Satan silenced. It shouts to him, "Stay back devil! I'm armed with the truth of God."[4]

(I encourage you to download Kyle's fantastic, free app, Shut Up Devil!, which is available in the Apple and Android App stores.)

3. Stand Firm

"And see, now I go bound in the spirit to Jerusalem, not knowing the things that will happen to me there, except that the Holy Spirit testifies in every city, saying that chains and tribulations await me. But none of these things move me; nor do I count my life dear to myself, so that I may finish my race with joy, and the ministry which I received from the Lord Jesus, to testify to the gospel of the grace of God." (Acts 20:22-25)

The future looked bleak. Paul was heading back to Jerusalem for what would become his arrest, his final trip to Rome, and ultimately his death. Many of Paul's colleagues warned him not to go to Jerusalem. The prophet Agabus held Paul's belt and prophesied,

> *"So shall the Jews in Jerusalem bind the man who owns this belt and deliver him into the hands of the Gentiles."*
> *(Acts 21:11)*

Yet Paul was undeterred. It was clear to him what he must do, what the Lord called him to do. And nothing anyone said or did would deter him from the journey.

He stood firm, even unto death.

It is highly unlikely that anything you ever stand for in your business might lead to your death. Yet even if it did, if the Lord called you to do it, it is ours to do without question.

In today's enemy-led marketplace, anything you attempt for the work of the Lord will be challenged, either in your spirit or in the workplace. Count on it.

Now is the time to stand firm, resting in the peace you have, knowing that the angel armies are at your back, the Word is in your heart and in your mouth, and the victory is ultimately the Lord's.

If the decision is…

- Small (e.g. which exit to take) – Stand firm!
- Big – Stand firm!
- Risky in the eyes of the world – Stand firm!
- Totally on your own witness – Stand firm!

Just like Paul.

One More Thing

Just like the big announcements made famous by the leaders of Apple, "Oh, there's one more thing."

The *one more thing* to stand firm is to put on the full armor of God (Ephesians 6:10-20). Paul mentioned "stand" three times in these verses so that we would be ready to block and destroy the wiles the enemy tosses at us.

As I previously mentioned in Section 4.5, "Armor Up," the earlier you put on the full armor of God, the more prepared you will be for the ultimate enemy attacks.

And in the end, you will not be moved!

Don't Be Moved Action Plan

Take time right now to complete this action plan. Keep it handy.

1. Stay on Focus – List 3-5 potential "squirrels" that could take you off focus from your most important goals. Just by recording them, you help yourself to not allow them to hinder your progress.

Squirrel #1:

Squirrel #2:

Squirrel #3:

Squirrel #4:

Squirrel #5:

2. Speak Back – Write down 3-5 verses you need to remember and memorize to exhort you to stay on focus and speak back to the enemy.

Verse #1:

Verse #2:

Verse #3:

Verse #4:

Verse #5:

3. Stand Firm – In your own words, create 3-5 personalized "Stand Firm" statements you can claim and speak out as needed. For example, one of my *Stand Firm* statements is simply like Paul shouted: "I will not be moved!"

Statement #1:

Statement #2:

Statement #3:

Statement #4:

Statement #5:

4. One More Thing –

"Therefore take up the whole armor of God, that you may be able to with-stand in the evil day, and having done all, to stand. Stand therefore, having girded your waist with truth, having put on the breastplate of righteousness, and having shod your feet with the preparation of the gos-pel of peace; above all, taking the shield of faith with which you will be able to quench all the fiery darts of the wicked one. And take the helmet of salvation, and the sword of the Spirit, which is the word of God."
~Ephesians 6:13-17

Write-below the six pieces of the armor of God. Purpose in your heart that, for one month, as you wake up or drive to work, you will speak these out loud with a declaration that you are fully ar-mored up and ready for the battle ahead. Not only will this give power and confidence to you, it will warn the enemy that he has no place in your business, and if he is foolish enough to try to wiggle into it, you will bind and cast him out in the Name of Jesus!

The Full Armor

1.

2.

3.

4.

5.

6.

5.6 PRAY BOLD PRAYERS

Bold (adj): not afraid of danger or difficult situations; very confident in a way that may seem rude or foolish; showing or requiring a fearless daring spirit

Joshua had been winning battle after battle, defeating every army God told him to fight. One time, God told him to march all night and prepare to battle against five kings joining forces. But by the end of the day, the battle was not over. So Joshua, desperately desiring to finish the battle in complete victory, prayed,

> *"At that time Joshua spoke to the Lord in the day when the Lord gave the Amorites over to the sons of Israel, and he said in the sight of Israel, 'Sun, stand still at Gibeon, and moon, in the Valley of Aijalon.' And the sun stood still, and the moon stopped, until the nation took vengeance on their enemies. Is this not written in the Book of Jashar? The sun stopped in the midst of heaven and did not hurry to set for about a whole day."*
> (Joshua 10:12-13)

Joshua's army defeated their enemies through God's answer to a powerful prayer of boldness.

Over the years, it's been far easier for me to pray bold prayers for my wife, son, family, friends, pastor, and church. But it was uncomfortable to do so for my business.

Sure, I've always prayed for my business. It's easy to pray for more contracts, better-paying customers, the turnaround of a wayward employee, or even for the Lord to help dismiss that ridiculous lawsuit. And who hasn't prayed to get out of a huge mess we created (probably from not being Spirit-led from the beginning).

I am by no means diminishing the importance of these basic prayers or any other prayers for our businesses. The Lord hears the prayers of His children. What I do exhort you to do is to shift your prayers into a much higher gear, a gear literally to unleash the supernatural favor of God on your business!

> *"'Now, Lord, look on their threats, and grant to Your servants that with all boldness they may speak Your word, by stretching out Your hand to heal, and that signs and wonders may be done through the name of Your holy Servant Jesus.' And when they had prayed, the place where they were assembled together was shaken; and they were all filled with the Holy Spirit, and they spoke the word of God with boldness."*
> (Acts 4:29-31)

This is the first recorded prayer of the new church apostles, just days after Pentecost and minutes after having been threatened by the religious leaders to cease and desist!

Facing severe trials, beatings, and even death, the first apostles easily could have offered safe, unassuming, just-help-us-get-through-this-situation prayers and then quietly gone about their business. *We sure do not want to offend, upset, or cause a ruckus.*

They could have taken a safer, easier route, but they chose to go another way. They chose to shift their prayers into a higher, more Spirit-filled gear. They chose to boldly go before the throne and ask for more!

Their house was shaken. Their confidence was stirred. Their faith was increased.

And we still see and feel the results: supernatural growth and eternal impact!

Recently, I started my shift beyond safe, normal, and expected prayers into a higher level of deep, dynamic, and bold prayers for my business. There is a huge difference.

So, what might this shift sound like? Here are three examples.

> **Safe:** "God, help me make payroll this month."
> **Shift:** "God, release your ministering angels to bring me $100,000 increase this month's revenue in Jesus' name!"

> **Safe:** "God, show us how to jump our sales 20% this year."
> **Shift:** "God, bless me with a two-fold (or five-fold or ten-fold or more) increase in our business in Jesus' name!"

> **Safe:** "God, help my CFO, Tony, repair his marriage."
> **Shift:** "God, supernaturally invade Tony's and his wife's home and hearts so they will have a powerful encounter with your Spirit and permanent healing of their marriage in Jesus' name!"

Please, let's not get into a discussion of the theological soundness of these prayers. Just read and sense the differences: the depth, the potential impact, and the boldness!

- Which prayers would you rather pray for your business?

- Which prayers would you rather your employees pray for your business?

- Which prayer do you think God might be more inclined to honor?

There are three things you need to do to pray bolder prayers: *ask, believe,* and *expect.*

1: Ask

"And Jabez called on the God of Israel saying, 'Oh, that You would bless me indeed, and enlarge my territory, that Your hand would be with me, and that You would keep me from evil, that I may not cause pain!' So God granted him what he requested."

~1 Chronicles 4:10

Blessing. Territory. Power. Protection.

These are the four areas the righteous man, Jabez, asked of God. For too many people, this prayer appears selfish. To 2%ers, this should become a model for our bolder business prayers.

In his best-selling book, *The Prayer of Jabez*, Bruce Wilkinson writes,

> *"If you're doing your business God's way, it's not only right to ask for more, but He is waiting for you to ask. Your business is the territory God has entrusted to you. He wants you to accept it as a significant opportunity to touch individual lives, the business community, and the larger world for His glory. Asking Him to enlarge that opportunity brings Him only delight."*[5]

Imagine, God actually is waiting for you to ask Him.

Have you ever waited for your child to ask you to take him or her to the park, or to a movie, or to help him or her learn how to drive? Often, our internal response is, "Finally!" It was your desire all along, yet the best thing to do was to wait until he or she asked.

That's exactly God does. As Dr. Wilkinson says, "Your business is the territory God has entrusted to you." So it is only right that He is ready and willing to bless your efforts in a big way.

He's waiting for you to ask, so you might as well be bold about it!

2: Expect

"So God granted him what he requested."
~*1 Chronicles 4:10b*

Did you catch God's reply to Jabez' request, or did you skip over it like I did for so many years?

As 2%ers, we tend to focus on the over-the-top boldness of Jabez—directly asking God for more business, bigger territory, a stronger hedge, and deliverance from the enemy's potential attacks—but miss the significance of God's response.

He granted Jabez what he requested!

He said, "Sure... here it is. I'm glad you finally asked!"

Jesus and James taught us the same thing:

> *"Ask, and it will be given to you; seek, and you will find; knock, and it will be opened to you. For everyone who asks receives, and he who seeks finds, and to him who knocks it will be opened."* (Matthew 7:7-8)

> *"Yet you do not have because you do not ask."*
> (James 4:2b)

I refuse to dive into a deep theological diatribe on what God blesses and what He does not. You can study that elsewhere. For now, simply realize that Jabez is described as an honorable, righteous man (1 Chronicles 4:9).

As a 2%er, you have inherited the righteousness of Christ (1 Corinthians 1:30). Therefore, in God's eyes, you are just as righteous as Jabez. Therefore, you can expect supernatural outcomes for your business in response to your bold prayers.

It is not enough to just ask. You must also expect!

3: Believe

"Delight yourself also in the Lord, and He shall give you the desires of your heart. Commit your way to the Lord, trust also in Him, and He shall bring it to pass."

~Psalm 37:4-5

You must be bold enough to ask.

You must be bold enough to expect what you ask for.

You must also be bold enough to believe your prayers are worthy enough to be answered.

It is time for all 2%ers—every one of us—to believe it is our time to transform the marketplace.

It's time to increase our borders!

It's time to witness supernatural growth!

It's time to shift our prayers into a much higher level of boldness!

> *"But Jesus looked at them and said to them, 'With men this is impossible, but with God all things are possible.'"*
> *(Matthew 19:26)*

It's time.

One Precaution

"The only time my prayers are never answered is on the golf course."

~Billy Graham

This is my favorite golf quote ever. Man, this is so true.

So to help all my fellow golfers, here is a simple, bold, golf prayer you can to add to your pre-round routine.

"Lord, may all my drives find the fairway, all my first putts drop in the cup, and all my wayward shots super-naturally walk on the water just like Jesus! Amen!"

Let me know if this prayer works for you. To see how it is working for me, check my Facebook page or read my blog. I'll post some updates for you.

Pray Bold Prayers Action Plan

Take time now to record three areas in which you sense the Spirit is urging you to pray more boldly. Jot down what your safe prayer could be. Then, get with the Spirit, and ask Him how He desires you to pray your bold prayers!

I would LOVE for you to send your bold prayers to me privately so I can seek a co-witness with you. Just e-mail them to Jim@DrJimHarris.com. I will reply. Confidentially.

Focus #1: _____

Safe:

Shift:

Focus #2: _____

Safe:

Shift:

Focus #3: _____

Safe:

Shift:

This workspace reserved ONLY for golfers!

Golf Focus #1: _____

Safe:

Shift:

Golf Focus #2: _____

Safe:

Shift:

[1] Kyle Winkler, *Silence Satan: Shutting Down the Enemy's Attacks, Threats, Lies, and Accusations* (Lake Mary, FL: Passio, 2014), 161.

[2] Ibid., 162.

[3] Ibid., 163.

[4] Ibid., 165.

[5] Dr. Bruce H. Wilkinson, *The Prayer of Jabez: Breaking Through to the Blessed Life* (Sisters, OR: Multnomah Publishers, 2000), 31-32.

CHAPTER 6

KEEP IT GOING

"And let us not grow weary while doing good, for in due season we shall reap if we do not lose heart."

~Galatians 6:9

To begin something is easy.
   To keep it going… that's the tough part.
   This chapter offers five areas to help you keep your momentum as you begin to release your unfair advantage in your market.

6.1. REMEMBER THE BENEFITS

benefit (n): a good or helpful result or effect; an act of kindness; something that promotes well-being

Two years ago, I was diagnosed with right-shoulder "tendinosis with osteoarthritis acromioclavicular joint and small joint effusion." The point: my torn rotator hurt like the dickens! The pain was so great I could not reach for my handkerchief in my right back pants pocket. At night, as I tried to fall asleep, it felt like a spike was being driven into my right upper arm. At no time could I extend my right arm above my shoulder.

When the orthopedic surgeon at the world-famous Andrews Clinic in Gulf Breeze, FL instructed me to begin a rehab and exercise routine, it was very easy for me to be convinced of the benefits. I was a walking pain bomb, so anything was better than my continued suffering.

I breezed through two weeks of light physical therapy and then began an aggressive, at-home, strength-building routine supervised by a former college football coach and close friend, John Saxon. I saw quick and dramatic improvement, gained upper-body strength, and significantly lowered the pain.

Once I got into a morning routine of five-day-a-week training, remembering the benefits was obvious. For the first time in my life, I actually could see "bumps" (muscles) building on my biceps and triceps. Having always been a thin-framed guy, I was now at 60+ years old and gaining just a little bit of real muscle.

Remember the benefits of training? Easy. Just look at my records of my weekly sheets of goals and measurements and accelerated exercises. The notebook is filled with the benefits of my exercise. Beyond that, I now feel so much stronger, more energetic, more focused, and more confident. By remembering and sensing the obvious benefits of training, I still keep on going and growing.

The same is true with unleashing your unfair competitive advantage.

It's Easy to Forget

"Our fathers in Egypt did not understand Your wonders; they did not remember the multitude of Your mercies."

~Psalm 106:7

Let's admit it: It is far too easy to forget the good things (benefits) in your business life and remember the bad. Like mine, your day-to-day leadership easily can be filled with ruts, routines, rituals, and never-ending challenges and frustrations that force you to focus only on the here-and-now—or, maybe, a little into next week.

Too often, the "tyranny of the urgent" impedes on your every hour. The madness created in business today of always on, always connected, 24/7/365, non-stop expectations severely can weaken and distract you from remembering what happened last night... let alone last year.

We naturally tend to remember the failures and struggles more than the victories and triumphs. Ever wonder who brings these natural failures to our remembrance? Not the Holy Spirit... that's for sure!

Because the enemy is the prince of this business world and desires above all to kill, steal, and destroy anything good—especially targeting supernaturally-empowered, Spirit-filled professionals— it's no wonder we so easily forget even the blessed times when the Holy Spirit has moved within and throughout our businesses.

I fall prey to this as well. I've learned it takes concerted effort for me to stop, reflect, and remember the ways in which the Lord directed me in my business through His Holy Spirit.

Quick... jot down how the Holy Spirit has benefited your business or career:

10 years ago?

5 years ago?

Last year?

This year?

Last week?

Yesterday?

It's easy to forget. Even though the Holy Spirit gives us a sound mind (2 Timothy 1:7), it is still far too easy to forget how often the Lord—through His Spirit—has guided, protected, and prospered you in your work.

To keep your new momentum going, let's make it easier to remember the good.

Your Top Ten Benefits List

"But these things I have told you, that when the time comes, you may remember that I told you of them."
~John 14:16

Take a 10-minute break right now. Turn off your phone, your computer, and at most, softly play some worship music in the background. Get quiet. Turn inside yourself and get in touch with the Holy Spirit. Ask the Spirit to help you list 10 benefits of unleashing the Holy Spirit in your business.

Your list likely will be different than anyone else's. The Holy Spirit will speak to you about your unique role in your unique company in your unique environment with your unique gifts and talents. It may include everything from Bible verses, words of encouragement, actions, measurable returns, and so much more.

The Top Ten benefits of unleashing the Holy Spirit in my business include…

1.

2.

3.

4.

5.

6.

7.

8.

9.

10.

Well done. Now you need to remember this list.

A 30-Day Benefits Challenge

"I will remember the works of the Lord; Surely I will remember Your wonders of old."

~Psalms 77:11

Keep this list handy for the next 30 days. Refer to it at least two times a day.

Make a reminder list in your phone. Write each item on a notecard. Post the card on your bathroom mirror, your dashboard, or in your *to do* list. Put this list anywhere that keeps it in front of you.

By soaking this list into your spirit over the next 30 days, you will remind and motivate yourself more quickly to leverage the power of the Holy Spirit for maximum impact throughout your business.

Power of Benefits

"And you shall remember the Lord your God, for it is He who gives you power to get wealth, that He may establish His covenant which He swore to your fathers, as it is this day."

~Deuteronomy 8:18

The Lord gives you the power to flourish in your business. Your benefits list will serve as a constant reminder that His Spirit is working through you to defeat your enemies, move your mountains. It will remind you that God deserves all the glory.

6.2. KEEP A RECORD

"It seemed good to me also, having had perfect understanding of all things from the very first, to write to you an orderly account, most excellent Theophilus, that you may know the certainty of those things in which you were instructed."

~Luke 1:3-4

In the previous section, "Remember the Benefits," you took a look back in time as a way to remind yourself of how the Holy Spirit has impacted you in your business in the past.

"Keep a Record" is future-focused. It is an exhortation to begin a record-keeping system in which you can notate, reflect, and grow a warehouse of the movement of the Holy Spirit in your business.

My Three-Journal System

My record system includes three 5"x8" lined leather journals: a business journal, a spiritual journal, and a sermon notes journal.

My brown business journal includes an open area for general business note-taking as well as sections for my clients, book and blog ideas, and business impact records.

My black journal is my personal spiritual growth journal in which I record daily insights from the Holy Spirit, Bible study notes, and sermon notes from my church.

My third journal, also black, is dedicated solely to notes from listening to sermon podcasts of great Bible teachers like Keith Moore, Tony White, Dan Mohler, and more.

For me, this system works. While working, I keep my brown business journal handy. When I attend services or go to pray during the week at my house of prayer, I take my personal spiritual journal. When I listen to podcasts or watch sermons on TV or the internet, I take notes in the sermons' journal.

Weekly, I review these journals, highlighting in yellow major revelations, prophetic words, insights, ideas, and anything the Spirit urges me to recall.

One of my favorite times is to pull out these journals and just read the yellow highlights. For me, that is the real power of my system. It is an orderly account of how the Spirit has been guiding me in all areas of my life, and it helps me remember the benefits of continuing this journey.

Ultimately, all these journals and notes blend together in my spirit to help edify and exhort me toward higher levels of Holy Spirit impact through my business.

The preaching notes so often fit into a business concept the Lord leads me to share.

The revelations I glean from my prayer time and devotionals launches my spirit into a higher level of connectedness and insight.

The business journal helps me align my spirit with His Spirit into where He desires me to journey.

This may be overkill for you, but it works for me. Discover what works for you.

Here's a Great Idea

Why not ask the Holy Spirit what record-keeping system is best for you? (Key #1: Practice!)

Hey, He already knows!

Whatever it is, just start. Over time, you will refine a system that works well for you, one that is sustainable and that encourages you to stay the course.

That's the point. Get started, and don't stop!

As you do, you'll look back and see how many times the Holy Spirit has impacted your business ventures, your people, your customers, and more.

Then, you'll keep going and going and going and...

6.3. NOT ALL THINGS SPIRITUAL ARE OF GOD

"For such are false apostles, deceitful workers, transforming themselves into apostles of Christ. And no wonder! For Satan himself transforms himself into an angel of light."

~*2 Corinthians 11:13-15*

The Spirit led me to include this cautionary note: not everything spiritual is of God.

The enemy is the father of lies, and there is no truth in him (John 8:44-45). As you commit yourself to releasing the power of the Holy Spirit in your business, the enemy will do everything he can to stop, delay, discourage, and even destroy you.

Here are three ways to keep the enemy at bay.

1. Study the Truth

We've all heard the story of how federal agents and financial professionals are trained to discern a counterfeit bill. They do not study the counterfeit bills, but rather, immerse themselves into only studying the real bills. Why? So when they see any deviation from what they know is the truth, they immediately can spot the fake, and the deceit is ended.

Stay constantly in the Word (how many times have you heard THAT in your life). Let the truth become second nature, your foundation for judging all things.

The better you know the truth, the easier it will be to discern a lie, a deception, or any attempt of the enemy to deceive you.

2. Don't Focus Just on the Supernatural

Indeed, the Holy Spirit moves in supernatural ways. Our salvation is the most dramatic and obvious example. Yet I caution you not to look only for a supernatural manifestation of the Spirit at work.

Can the Spirit manifest Himself in supernatural ways in your workplace? Of course He can. But more often, he works in more subtle spiritual ways (e.g. a softening heart, lower interpersonal tensions, better teamwork, more grace and love and kindness, happier employees, and even more smiles in the office).

It is easy when learning about the power of the Holy Spirit to get caught up in looking only for the *supernatural* (e.g. a physical healing, spiritual deliverance from enemy oppression, etc.).

As Keith Moore says, "Do not dismiss the spiritual looking for the supernatural."

3. Does It Align?

"Be diligent to present yourself approved to God, a worker who does not need to be ashamed, rightly dividing the word of truth."
~2 Timothy 2:15

Check every spiritual thing you sense occurring in your workplace against the Word and the Witness.

If what you see and sense aligns with the Word and you have a Witness, it is the Spirit.

If what you see and sense does not align with the Word, and you have no Witness, it is of the enemy.

As you build your sensitivity to the ways and workings of the Holy Spirit in your workplace, you will learn to distinguish quickly His ways from the enemy's ways.

6.4. STAY COACHED UP

"A wise man will hear and increase learning, and a man of understanding will attain wise counsel."

~Proverbs 1:5

Here is my unabashed shout-out for you to work with a business coach, mentor, covenant group, and/or a spiritual advisor.

Any one of the four would be good.

Working with all four would be phenomenal!

One sad thing I've learned in my years of advising and coaching business leaders is only very, very few are open to being coached. They are too proud, too "busy," or too afraid of being held accountable.

However, those who seek professional and spiritual advisors possess a humble sprit that desires to learn, grow, and become all they were designed by God to be.

For years, I've had professional and spiritual coaches, mentors, and accountability groups that teach, guide, encourage, and keep me pointed in the right direction.

I practice what I preach.

We all need it... even book authors.

My 3-Step Coaching Accountability Formula

"And He said to them, 'He who has ears to hear, let him hear.'"

~Mark 4:9

Okay, I am about to give away one of my most powerful and simple coaching formulas, something so simple that many scoff at it.

Yet the business professionals who embrace this 3-step model have experienced transformational results in as little as 90 days.

After we determine the specific goals they need to achieve in the next 90 days, I challenge them to answer these three simple questions:

- What must you START doing?
- What must you STOP doing?
- What must you CONTINUE doing?

We discuss and clarify each thing listed to ensure it is achievable and challenging. Then, my role converts into an accountability partner to check progress, adjust, and help guide them to follow-through to completion.

Try it yourself. Below, note 2-5 things you need to *start, stop,* or *continue* doing to unleash your unfair competitive advantage.

What must I START doing?

1.

2.

3.

4.

5.

What must I STOP doing?

1.

2.

3.

4.

5.

What must I CONTINUE doing?

1.

2.

3.

4.

5.

Share your list with another 2%er. Ask that person to create his or her own list.

Better yet, if you are open, seek an unbiased professional coach, mentor, or advisor. Trust me... when you have a little "skin in the game," you will be far more likely to follow through on your commitments.

My Offer to You

If you would like to get started now, here is a free offer to you.

Confidentially e-mail your "Start-Stop-Continue List" to me at Jim@DrJimHarris.com. I will reply that I received your list and will offer any comments the Spirit prompts.

Then, *I will e-mail one time* within 30 days to check your progress.

Knowing you'll have one accountability check-in is enough for most of you to do something!

6.5. IT'S ALL ABOUT IMPACT

"Go therefore and make disciples of all the nations, baptizing them in the name of the Father and of the Son and of the Holy Spirit, teaching them to observe all things that I have commanded you; and lo, I am with you always, even to the end of the age. Amen."

~Matthew 28:19-20

In the end, it is all about impact. Our work on earth will be measured by how well we impact this fallen planet with the gospel.

> *"And being assembled together with them, He commanded them not to depart from Jerusalem, but to wait for the Promise of the Father, 'Which,' He said, 'you have heard from Me; for John truly baptized with water, but you shall be baptized with the Holy Spirit not many days from now.'" (Acts 1:4-5)*

You and I have the promise living inside us. It is a promise you can now better leverage in your workplace for the ultimate impact we all desire, which is to hear...

> *"'Well done, good and faithful servant; you were faithful over a few things, I will make you ruler over many things. Enter into the joy of your lord."* (Matthew 25:21)

I pray this book has helped you to take one step further into reaching your eternal impact.

THE ANSWER TO 1001 QUESTIONS

"The answer to 1001 questions is… BE LED!"
~Pastor Keith Moore

20 Key Verses

H ere are 20 key verses you need to memorize to help you unleash your unfair competitive advantage.

Keep these handy.

Bury these words deep in your heart.

*"Rejoice always, pray without ceasing, in everything give thanks; for
this is the will of God in Christ Jesus for you. Do not quench the Spirit."*

~1 Thessalonians 5:16-19

*"But none of these things move me; nor do I count my life dear to myself,
so that I may finish my race with joy, and the ministry which I received
from the Lord Jesus, to testify to the gospel of the grace of God."*

~Acts 20:24-25

*"The Spirit Himself bears witness with our spirit that we are children of
God."*

~Romans 8:16

*"Do not love the world or the things in the world. If anyone loves the
world, the love of the Father is not in him. For all that is in the world —
the lust of the flesh, the lust of the eyes, and the pride of life — is not of
the Father but is of the world."*

~1 John 2:15-16

"And I will pray the Father, and He will give you another Helper, that He may abide with you forever — the Spirit of truth, whom the world cannot receive, because it neither sees Him nor knows Him; but you know Him, for He dwells with you and will be in you."

~John 14:16-17

"For as many as are led by the Spirit of God, these are sons of God..."

~Romans 8:14

"To him the doorkeeper opens, and the sheep hear his voice; and he calls his own sheep by name and leads them out. And when he brings out his own sheep, he goes before them; and the sheep follow him, for they know his voice."

~John 10:3-4

"But as it is written: 'Eye has not seen, nor ear heard, Nor have entered into the heart of man, The things which God has prepared for those who love Him.' But God has revealed them to us through His Spirit. For the Spirit searches all things, yes, the deep things of God. For what man knows the things of a man except the spirit of the man which is in him? Even so no one knows the things of God except the Spirit of God."

~1 Corinthians 2:9-11

"Now we have received, not the spirit of the world, but the Spirit who is from God, that we might know the things that have been freely given to us by God."

~1 Corinthians 2:12

"However, when He, the Spirit of truth, has come, He will guide you into all truth; for He will not speak on His own authority, but whatever He hears He will speak and He will tell you things to come."

~John 16:13

"Trust in the Lord with all your heart, and lean not on your own under-standing. In all your ways acknowledge Him, and He shall direct your paths."

~*Proverbs 3:5-6*

"And do not be conformed to this world, but be transformed by the re-newing of your mind, that you may prove what is that good and acceptable and perfect will of God."

~*Romans 12:2*

"But My servant Caleb, because he has a different spirit in him and has followed Me fully, I will bring into the land where he went, and his de-scendants shall inherit it."

~*Numbers 14:24*

"And whatever you do, do it heartily, as to the Lord and not to men, knowing that from the Lord you will receive the reward of the inher-itance; for you serve the Lord Christ."

~*Colossians 3:23*

"For it seemed good to the Holy Spirit, and to us, to lay upon you no greater burden than these necessary things."

~*Acts 15:28*

"Ask, and it will be given to you; seek, and you will find; knock, and it will be opened to you."

~*Matthew 7:7*

"And do not grieve the Holy Spirit of God, by whom you were sealed for the day of redemption."

~*Ephesians 4:30*

"Rejoice always, pray without ceasing, in everything give thanks; for this is the will of God in Christ Jesus for you. Do not quench the Spirit."
~*1 Thessalonians 5:16-19*

"And Jabez called on the God of Israel saying, 'Oh, that You would bless me indeed, and enlarge my territory, that Your hand would be with me, and that You would keep me from evil, that I may not cause pain!' So God granted him what he requested."
~*1 Chronicles 4:10*

"And let us not grow weary while doing good, for in due season we shall reap if we do not lose heart."
~*Galatians 6:9*

And finally, remember…

"The only time my prayers are never answered is on the golf course."
~*Billy Graham*

ABOUT DR. JIM HARRIS

Dr. Jim Harris is President of The Jim Harris Group, an international speaking and advising firm dedicated to helping believers in business unleash their unfair advantage in the marketplace. He is the author of *The Impacter: A Parable on Transformational Leadership* and numerous other award winning business books.

His clients are a Who's Who in business, including Walmart, IBM, Best Buy, Verizon, Johnson & Johnson, Wells Fargo, Ford, and Walt Disney along with Malcolm Baldrige winners and INC 500 Fast Growth firms.

Dr. Jim is a sought-after speaker at Christian conferences and as a guest preacher. He serves on many Boards of Directors with marketplace and teaching ministries.

The Jim Harris Group
2015 Cameron Drive
Pensacola, FL 32505
850-476-6633
jim@drjimharris.com

Connect with Dr. Jim on…

Web www.DrJimHarris.com
Facebook:/DrJimHarris
Twitter: @DrJImHarris
LinkedIn: DrJimHarris

To purchase copies of *Our Unfair Advantage* in bulk, please contact High Bridge Books via www.HighBridgeBooks.com/contact.

BUSINESS SERVICES

For over 25 years, Dr. Jim has spoken to hundreds of audiences around the world on leadership and business best practices. From Fortune 500 firms to fast-growth entrepreneurial firms, his messages are filled with real-world truths and take-home value. He advises and coaches professionals in all walks of life from CEOs, VPs, managers, pastors, and growth-focused entrepreneurs.

- ✔ Keynotes / Workshops
- ✔ Conferences / Retreats
- ✔ One-On-One Coaching
- ✔ Team Coaching / Team Building
- ✔ Strategic Planning / Advising

DR. JIM HARRIS

To learn more or to schedule
Dr. Jim to speak at your next event...

- *Email info@DrJimHarris.com*
- *Visit www.DrJimHarris.com, or*
- *Call 850-476-6633*

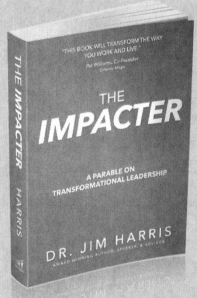

MINISTRY SERVICES

Dr. Jim is a seasoned ministry speaker and confidential advisor to ministers and their teams. From sermons to retreats, Dr. Jim brings a passion to impact disciples toward filling their eternal calling. His ministry experience ranges for leading multiple capital and spiritual campaigns for large churches, church strategic planning retreats, 20+ years leading Adult Bible studies, speaking at Pastor conferences and special prayer events.

- ✔ Business Outreach Conferences
- ✔ Guest Speaking and Preaching
- ✔ Staff Retreats
    (Visioning, Planning, Team Building)
- ✔ One-On-One Coaching
- ✔ Team Coaching

DR. JIM HARRIS

To learn more or to schedule
Dr. Jim to speak at your next event...

- *Email info@DrJimHarris.com*
- *Visit www.DrJimHarris.com, or*
- *Call 850-476-6633*

CPSIA information can be obtained at www.ICGtesting.com
Printed in the USA
LVOW08s0948090616

491553LV00002B/6/P